THE REMOVER OF DIFFICULTIES

In memory of my brother Gianni

The Remover of Difficulties

Reflections on the Prayer of the Báb

Enrico Ballerio

GR

GEORGE RONALD OXFORD

George Ronald, Publisher
Oxford
www.grbooks.com

A catalogue record for this book is available
from the British Library

ISBN 978-0-85398-609-6

Cover design: René Steiner, Steinergraphics.com

CONTENTS

Prologue: A Brief History   xiii

Introduction   1

Part I: 'Is There Any Remover of Difficulties Save God?'   5

1   Some Initial Considerations   7
2   The Creative Power of the Word of God   12
3   The Power and Purpose of Prayer   15
4   More on Prayer   22
5   The Purpose of Difficulties and of Overcoming Them   31
6   Types of Affliction   40
7   The Mystery of Sacrifice   50

Intermezzo: God Loves Laughter   59

Part II: 'Praised be God! He is God! All Are His Servants and All Abide by His Bidding!'   67

8   To Praise God   69
9   Overcoming Difficulties   72
10   The Value of Struggle   79
11   Service   83
12   Obedience and Submission   91
13   Joy and Pain   96

14 The Path that Leads to Happiness   101
15 Is There Room for Doubt?   109
16 A Short Summing Up . . .   114
17 . . . and a Conclusion   120

Bibliography   127
Notes and References   131

To my parents
who through their loving education in a healthy fear of God
have helped me to turn always and with faith to Him Who
removes the difficulties
that life inevitably reserves for us

And to my children
in the hope of having educated and watched over them as
precious trusts
assigned to me by a munificent Creator

ACKNOWLEDGEMENTS

To Him, Who in his infinite generosity has enabled this humble servant to express his sincere love in the form of words, gratitude and praise are first due.

My thanks go to May Hofman, without whose lively interest and refined translation from the Italian text, this little book would never have seen the light of day. I thank her for her commitment, for the useful advice generously offered and for having introduced me to the art of book publication.

Particular appreciation goes to my wife Silvana, who allowed me to dedicate the necessary time to writing the book, encouraging me even through constructive criticism which was very useful in honing my vision of life.

I thank my late brother Giovanni, and my sister Adelisa, who have always given me their trust, sustaining me in my shortcomings. Adelisa in particular assisted in refining parts of this book; among other things, the short biographical note about the author at the end of the book is hers.

And finally, my thanks go to the Bahá'í community of Asmara (Eritrea), which saw my spiritual birth and guided me in my first steps in this marvellous adventure of spiritual rebirth; to the Bahá'í community of Padova, which received me as a brother on my return to Italy; and to all those who have in some way offered their support and encouragement.

Know ye that trials and tribulations have,
from time immemorial,
been the lot of the chosen Ones of God and His beloved,
and such of His servants as are detached from all else but
Him . . .
Blessed are the steadfastly enduring,
they that are patient under ills and hardships,
who lament not over anything that befalleth them,
and who tread the path of resignation.
Bahá'u'lláh[1]

Place, in all circumstances, Thy whole trust in Thy
Lord, and fix Thy gaze upon Him . . .
Let God, Thy Lord, be Thy sufficing succourer
and helper.
Bahá'u'lláh[2]

(French, rotated, upper left)
Qui autre que Dieu dissipe les difficultés ? Loué soit Dieu ! Lui seul est Dieu ! Tous sont Ses serviteurs et tous dépendent de Son commandement.

(Spanish, rotated, upper right)
¿Quién libra de las dificultades salvo Dios? Di: ¡Alabado sea Dios! Él es Dios! Todos somos sus siervos y todos nos atenemos a su mandato.

هَلْ مِنْ
مُفَرِّجٍ غَيْرَ اللّٰهِ؟
قُلْ سُبْحَانَ اللّٰهِ،
هُوَ اللّٰهُ كُلٌّ عِبَادُهُ لَهُ
وَكُلٌّ بِأَمْرِهِ قَائِمُونَ.

Is there any Remover of difficulties Save God?

Say: Praised be God! He is God!

All are His servants,

And all abide by His bidding!

The Báb

Chi può rimuovere le difficoltà eccetto Dio?

Dite: Lodato sia Iddio! Egli è Dio!

Tutti sono i Suoi servi, e tutti stanno al Suo comando

(German, rotated, lower left)
Gibt es einen Befreier von Schwierigkeiten außer Gott? Sprich: Gelobt sei Gott! Er ist Gott! Alle sind Seine Diener und alle stehen unter Seinem Befehl.

(Portuguese, rotated, lower right)
Há quem remova as dificuldades, a não ser Deus? Dize: Louvado seja Deus! Ele é Deus! Todos são Seus servos e todos aquiescem a Seu mandamento.

PROLOGUE: A BRIEF HISTORY

Turning the pages of ancient books, looking at drawings and rare photographs, we seem to return in time to nineteenth-century Persia, beneath those sweet skies wrapped in a profound silence, to breathe in the warm scent of roses and to glance at the golden plains rich in verdant gardens.

A world that seems so far from our own, so remote – its actions frozen in time and place, environments now long gone. A world immersed in the atmosphere of revelation.

On the horizon, a city of merchants and poets, enpurpled by the red of the sunset to shades of blood, wrapped in the warm perfume of roses – Shiraz, a city like so many, immersed in its centuries-old torpor, always the same, always itself.

Inside its walls, time stood still on the evening of 22 May 1844, at that instant when a young Merchant announced to a fervent seeker from Karbila that he was the Sun in a new Dispensation, the Báb, the 'Gate' to the opening of the Revelation of 'Him Whom God Will Make Manifest'.[1]

These poetic lines by a sensitive and thoughtful writer seem to me the most fitting introduction to the presentation of this modest homage to Siyyid 'Alí-Muḥammad, the young Merchant of Shiraz known to history as the Báb.

About halfway through the last century, a group of journalists were invited to enter a newspaper competition. The task was to see who could write the most exciting headline that would in their opinion catch readers' attention. The winning headline, by a long way, consisted of just two words: 'Christ Returns!'

But in fact they were a century too late. Articles had already been published in the 1840s on the return of Christ, because it was at that time that followers of all the great revealed religions, and particularly Christians and Muslims on the basis of the many prophecies in their Sacred Texts, were fervently awaiting the Messiah. And so, how unsurprising it is to find that during those years – specifically on the evening of 22 May 1844 – that young merchant of Shiraz, unknown up to that moment, had made a staggering claim: he declared that this was the Day promised in the scriptures of the past, the day in which the Promised One of all religions would appear, the day of 'one shepherd and one flock'. The Bahá'í Writings tell us:

O My friends that dwell upon the dust! Haste forth unto your celestial habitation. Announce unto yourselves the joyful tidings: 'He Who is the Best-Beloved is come! He has crowned Himself with the glory of God's Revelation, and hath unlocked to the face of men the doors of His ancient Paradise.' Let all eyes rejoice, and let every ear be gladdened, for now is the time to gaze on His beauty, now is the fit time to hearken to His voice . . .[2]

In every age and cycle He hath, through the splendorous light shed by the Manifestations of His wondrous Essence, recreated all things, so that whatsoever reflecteth in the heavens and on the earth the signs of His glory may not be deprived of the outpourings of His mercy, nor despair of the showers of His favours. How all-compassing are the wonders of His boundless grace! Behold how they have pervaded the whole of creation. Such is their virtue that not a single atom in the entire universe can be found which does not declare the evidences of His might, which doth not glorify His holy Name, or is not expressive of the effulgent light of His unity.[3]

The Báb's life was short and tragic. Because of His words and teachings he was soon made prisoner and then martyred in the public square. The only historical parallel that can be found to His short and tumultuous life is the moving narration of the life and passion of Jesus Christ.

The Báb proclaimed Himself to be the Herald and precursor of One greater than Himself. His own mission was to close the Prophetic Cycle begun by Adam in order to bring mankind to God, preparing the way for the great Redeemer of the world announced by Christ and all the Messengers of the past – the Redeemer who would open a new Cycle, a new era.

Mírzá Ḥusayn 'Alí, who assumed the title Bahá'u'lláh (the Glory of God), publicly announced on 21 April 1863 in a garden on the outskirts of Baghdad that He was 'He Whom God shall make manifest', thus initiating the new Revelation. Bahá'ís, then, are those who recognize in Bahá'u'lláh the Manifestion of God for our era:

Verily I say, this is the Day in which mankind can behold the Face, and hear the Voice, of the Promised One. The Call of God hath been raised, and the light of His countenance hath been lifted up upon men. It behoveth every man to blot out the trace of every idle word from the tablet of his heart, and to gaze, with an open and unbiased mind, on the signs of His Revelation, the proofs of His Mission and the tokens of His glory . . .[4]

It is not, however, the purpose of this little book to present the Bahá'í Faith – since readers can turn to other sources of information that are far more detailed and authoritative – but, as previously mentioned, to render homage to the Báb through a simple and humble study of the short prayer revealed by Him, known universally as the Remover of Difficulties, and certainly the most well known and frequently recited by Bahá'ís all over the world.

INTRODUCTION

There are two prayers nearly every Bahá'í knows and, perhaps, recites more frequently than other prayers. Translated into every language imaginable and short enough to be easily learnt by heart, they nevertheless hold within their few words eternal and fundamental truths that express all the greatness and omnipotence of the Creator.

Revealed by the twin Manifestations of God for this time, they are, respectively: the prayer of the Báb known as the 'Remover of Difficulties' and the short Obligatory Prayer revealed by Bahá'u'lláh:

> Is there any Remover of difficulties save God? Say: Praised be God! He is God! All are His servants, and all abide by His bidding!
>
> *The Báb*

> I bear witness, O my God, that Thou hast created me to know Thee and to worship Thee. I testify, at this moment, to my powerlessness and to Thy might, to my poverty and to thy wealth.
>
> There is none other God but Thee, the Help in Peril, the Self-Subsisting.
>
> *Bahá'u'lláh*

It is easy to discern in these two prayers certain noteworthy parallels in both expression and content.

To the verse in the prayer of the Báb: 'Is there any Remover of difficulties save God?' Bahá'u'lláh responds that it is God Who is 'the Help in Peril'. The verse: 'Praised be God!' is rendered even more motiving and affirmative by the words: 'I bear witness, O my God, that Thou hast created me to know Thee and to worship Thee,' and the incisive affirmation of faith by the Báb: 'He is God!' is reiterated by Bahá'u'lláh in even more exclusive terms: 'There is none other God but Thee . . . the Self-Subsisting.' And finally: 'All are His servants, and all abide by His bidding' might well correspond to the affirmation of faith: 'I testify, at this moment, to my powerlessness and to Thy might, to my poverty and to thy wealth' – indeed, the servant is weak and poverty-stricken before his Lord, and thus it is to Him that he turns in obedience to His command.

Nobody really knows how or when the Báb revealed this short prayer. The most accepted hypothesis, and the one considered most likely by the worldwide Bahá'í community, is that the Báb revealed it for his beloved wife, as the following quotation from Nabíl's Narrative, *The Dawn-Breakers*, suggests:

> The second Naw-Rúz after the declaration of the Báb's Mission . . . found the Báb still in Shíráz enjoying, under circumstances of comparative tranquillity and ease, the blessings of undisturbed association with His family and kindred. Quietly and unceremoniously, He celebrated the festival of Naw-Rúz in His own home, and, in accordance with His invariable custom, bountifully conferred upon both His mother and His wife the marks of His affection and favour . . .
>
> The mother of the Báb failed at first to realize the significance of the Mission proclaimed by her Son . . . As she

approached the end of her life, however, she was able to perceive the inestimable quality of that Treasure which she had conceived and given to the world. It was Bahá'u'lláh who eventually enabled her to discover the value of that hidden Treasure which had lain for so many years concealed from her eyes . . . She acknowledged the truth of the Cause and remained, until the closing years of the thirteenth century A.H.[1882], when she departed this life, fully aware of the bountiful gifts which the Almighty had chosen to confer upon her.

The wife of the Báb, unlike His mother, perceived at the earliest dawn of His Revelation the glory and uniqueness of His Mission and felt from the very beginning the intensity of its force. No one except Ṭáhirih, among the women of her generation, surpassed her in the spontaneous character of her devotion nor excelled the fervour of her faith. To her the Báb confided the secret of His future sufferings, and unfolded to her eyes the significance of the events that were to transpire in His Day. He bade her not to divulge this secret to His mother and counselled her to be patient and resigned to the will of God. He entrusted her with a special prayer, revealed and written by Himself, the reading of which, He assured her, would remove her difficulties and lighten the burden of her woes. 'In the hour of your perplexity,' He directed her, 'recite this prayer ere you go to sleep. I Myself will appear to you and will banish your anxiety.' Faithful to His advice, every time she turned to Him in prayer, the light of His unfailing guidance illumined her path and resolved her problems.[1]

Thus, from the moment when Nabíl wrote the words: 'He entrusted her with a special prayer...the reading of which... *would remove her difficulties...*' Bahá'ís have always accepted the idea that this could mean the prayer 'Is there any Remover of difficulties…'.

PART ONE

'IS THERE ANY REMOVER
OF DIFFICULTIES
SAVE GOD?'

Happy the days that have been consecrated
to the remembrance of God,
and blessed the hours which have been spent
in praise of Him Who is the All-Wise.[1]

Lament not in your hours of trial,
neither rejoice therein;
seek ye the Middle Way which is the remembrance
of Me in your afflictions and reflection over that
which may befall you in future. Thus informeth you He Who
is the Omniscient, He Who is aware.[2]

1

SOMEINITIALCONSIDERATIONS

This short prayer revealed by the Báb is recited in many circumstances – and obviously, particularly in difficult moments.

In Bahá'í meetings it is sometimes recited by each participant in turn, while at the individual level, some recite it nine times, others 95 or even 500 times when things are particularly difficult. Nothing stands in the way of Bahá'í friends doing whatever they like in this respect. Systematic repetition of a verse when one is praying in one's own room can be favourable to meditation, if carried out with purity of intent. All the same, it is useful to remember the following:

1. This prayer has the power of all revealed prayer, but it is not included in those that have the 'special potency and significance' explained in the following letter written on behalf of Shoghi Effendi:

> These daily obligatory prayers, together with a few other specific ones, such as the Healing Prayer, the Tablet of Aḥmad, have been invested by Bahá'u'lláh with a special potency and significance, and should therefore be accepted as such and be recited by the believers with unquestioning faith and confidence, that through them they may enter into a much closer communion with God, and identify themselves more fully with His laws and precepts.[3]

Nevertheless, the Báb's words: 'In the hour of your perplexity, recite this prayer ere you go to sleep. I Myself will appear to you and will banish your anxiety,'⁴ although specifically addressed to his wife, may give us the hope that, by extension, the prayer may have the same effect on one who, finding himself 'in affliction or grief', will read it 'with absolute sincerity', as Bahá'u'lláh says about the Tablet of Aḥmad – these being the essential conditions in which God will hear his prayer, 'dispel his sadness, solve his difficulties and remove his afflictions'.⁵

2. In a letter addressed to a believer who had asked how many times it was necessary to repeat this prayer in order to obtain the maximum result (always bearing in mind the fundamental condition of 'sincerity' in reciting it), Shoghi Effendi's secretary replied on his behalf: 'Concerning the prayer for difficulty revealed by the Báb; he wishes me to inform you that it is not accompanied by any instructions for its recital.'⁶

In addition, in November 1971 the Universal House of Justice wrote to a National Spiritual Assembly as follows:

> . . . you have quoted the Báb's prayer for the removal of difficulties and have added: 'Bahá'u'lláh has said to repeat this prayer 500 times by day and by night that it may aid us to recognize Him and our souls will be illumined'.
>
> The above statement gives the impression that the repetition of the said prayer 500 times is one of the prescribed devotionals of the Faith, and has a specified effect on the believer who observes this form of prayer.
>
> We do not feel it is justified to infer such conclusions from the reference in 'God Passes By', page 119, which you mention. The passage in question obviously refers to a specific circumstance in the life of Bahá'u'lláh in Baghdád before the declaration of His Mission, and should not be

presented to the believers as one of the prescribed observances of the faith.[7]

The quotation from the words of Bahá'u'lláh in *God Passes By* mentioned above reads as follows:

> Bid them recite: 'Is there any Remover of difficulties save God? Say: Praised be God! He is God! All are His servants, and all abide by His bidding!' Tell them to repeat it five hundred times, nay, a thousand times, by day and by night, sleeping and waking, that haply the Countenance of Glory may be unveiled to their eyes, and tiers of light descend upon them.[8]

This is similar to what the Báb told his wife: 'In the hour of your perplexity, recite this prayer ere you go to sleep. I Myself will appear to you and will banish your anxiety.'

A moment's reflection on Bahá'u'lláh's instruction: 'Tell them to repeat it five hundred times, nay, a thousand times, by day and by night, *sleeping and waking* . . .' will show us that this seems impossible to carry out – at least, unless we recite the revealed verse (whether once or a thousand times) with such absolute sincerity, devotion and love that every single cell in our body is permeated with it, and every one of our thoughts, sleeping or waking, revolves around it.

3. Both the Guardian and the Universal House of Justice have always cautioned the believers against creating rites of any kind, while recognizing the freedom of every single individual to express private devotion in whatever way seems appropriate to him. We cite here the following letter written on behalf of the Universal House of Justice to the National Spiritual Assembly of Bolivia on 16 October 1979:

A dogma is a principle, tenet or teaching, especially an authoritative teaching, and in these senses it is apparent that the Faith has 'dogmas'. The word is also used, however, to describe that body of rigid doctrines that have accumulated in a religion after the passing of its Founder; such man-made dogmas are entirely absent from the Bahá'í Faith, nor can it ever acquire them.

Concerning rituals, the beloved Guardian's secretary wrote on his behalf to an individual believer on 24 June 1949:

'Bahá'u'lláh has reduced all ritual and form to an absolute minimum in His Faith. The few forms that there are – like those associated with the two longer obligatory daily prayers, are only symbols of the inner attitude. There is a wisdom in them, and a great blessing but we cannot force ourselves to understand or feel these things, that is why He gave us also the very short and simple prayer, for those who did not feel the desire to perform the acts associated with the other two.'

Thus it can be seen that the Faith has certain simple rites prescribed by Bahá'u'lláh, such as the obligatory prayers, the marriage ceremony and the laws for the burial of the dead, but its teachings warn against developing them into a system of uniform and rigid rituals incorporating man-made forms and practices, such as exist in other religions where rituals usually consist of elaborate ceremonial practices performed by a member of the clergy. In another letter written on behalf of the Guardian his secretary stated:

'In these days the friends should, as much as possible, demonstrate through their deeds the independence of the

Holy Faith of God, and its freedom from the customs, rituals and practices of a discredited and abrogated past.' (Translated from the Persian)

In freeing the believers from the religious rituals of the past and from those customs which are contrary to the Bahá'í principles, the institutions of the Faith should be careful not to press the friends to arbitrarily discard those local traditions which are harmless and often colourful characteristics of particular peoples and tribes. In 'The World Order of Bahá'u'lláh', on page 41, we read:

'Let there be no misgivings as to the animating purpose of the world-wide Law of Bahá'u'lláh. Far from aiming at the subversion of the existing foundations of society, it seeks to broaden its basis, to remould its institutions in a manner consonant with the needs of an ever-changing world. It can conflict with no legitimate allegiances, nor can it undermine essential loyalties. Its purpose is neither to stifle the flame of a sane and intelligent patriotism in men's hearts, nor to abolish the system of national autonomy so essential if the evils of excessive centralization are to be avoided. It does not ignore, nor does it attempt to suppress, the diversity of ethnical origins, of climate, of history, of language and tradition, of thought and habit, that differentiate the peoples and nations of the world . . .'[9]

Furthermore, in replying to a believer who had asked clarification regarding the duty to recite prayers nine times, the Guardian's secretary wrote on his behalf on 26 November 1939:

There is no obligation for a believer to recite always any prayer nine times. Ritualism is certainly to be avoided in all matters affecting Bahá'í worship . . .[10]

2

THE CREATIVE POWER OF THE WORD OF GOD

Irrespective of whether this prayer is invested with special power and significance or not, the fundamental fact remains that, like all revealed prayers, Tablets and Sacred Text, it is the Word of God and as such endowed with creative power. In the words of Adib Taherzadeh:

> The Word of God is the noblest form of the creation of God and it stands far above the comprehension of man. Bahá'u'lláh has warned us in a Tablet never to compare the creation of the 'Word' with the creation of other things. He states that each one of the words of God is like a mirror through which the attributes of God are reflected, and that through the Word of God all creation has come into being. The Revelation of Bahá'u'lláh, like that of the Báb, is the Word of God for this age and is, in like manner, creative.[1]

Bahá'u'lláh Himself writes about this:

> Every word that proceedeth out of the mouth of God is endowed with such potency as can instil new life into every human frame, if ye be of them that comprehend this truth. All the wondrous works ye behold in this world have

been manifested through the operation of His supreme and most exalted Will, His wondrous and inflexible Purpose. Through the mere revelation of the word 'Fashioner', issuing forth from His lips and proclaiming His attribute to mankind, such power is released as can generate, through successive ages, all the manifold arts which the hands of man can produce. This, verily, is a certain truth. No sooner is this resplendent word uttered, than its animating energies, stirring within all created things, give birth to the means and instruments whereby such arts can be produced and perfected. All the wondrous achievements ye now witness are the direct consequences of the Revelation of this Name. In the days to come, ye will, verily, behold things of which ye have never heard before. Thus hath it been decreed in the Tablets of God, and none can comprehend it except them whose sight is sharp. In like manner, the moment the word expressing My attribute 'The Omniscient' issueth forth from My mouth, every created thing will, according to its capacity and limitations, be invested with the power to unfold the knowledge of the most marvellous sciences, and will be empowered to manifest them in the course of time at the bidding of Him Who is the Almighty, the All-Knowing. Know thou of a certainty that the Revelation of every other Name is accompanied by a similar manifestation of Divine power. Every single letter proceeding out of the mouth of God is indeed a mother letter, and every word uttered by Him Who is the Well Spring of Divine Revelation is a mother word, and His Tablet a Mother Tablet. Well is it with them that apprehend this truth.[2]

And Taherzadeh continues:

The words which the Manifestations of God utter are the outer form of spiritual forces born of the Revelation of God. The innermost reality latent within the Word is limitless in its potentialities. It belongs to the world of God and is not fully comprehended by man, whose finite mind is only capable of grasping to a limited degree the meaning, the power and the creativeness of the Word.

The Word of God can be likened to the rays of the sun which carry its energy. Their intensity in close proximity to the sun is so great that no living creature can sustain their energy in outer space. Yet the same rays, traversing space and passing the atmosphere and layers of cloud, shed a limited portion of their energy on the surface of the earth. Similarly, in this world, the Word of God reveals a limited measure of its spiritual truth and meaning to the mind of man, who, by reason of his finite form is not capable of comprehending these in their fullness . . . the Manifestations Who reveal this Word are aware of its full potency and significance.[3]

The prayers revealed by the Manifestations to man, so that they may serve as a means enabling him to turn his own heart toward God, cannot but be endowed with a particular significance and power. 'Abdu'l-Bahá writes:

The wisdom of prayer is this: That it causeth a connection between the servant and the True One, because in that state man with all heart and soul turneth his face towards His Highness the Almighty, seeking His association and desiring His love and compassion.[4]

3

THE POWER AND PURPOSE OF PRAYER

We learn from the Bahá'í Writings that there are three fundamental levels of reality: the world of God, a world of Absolute
Unity wholly inaccessible to man; at the other extreme, the
world of creation to which man belongs; and an intermedi-
ate world which operates between the two others. This is the
world of the Kingdom, of the Spirit, or Logos, or the Word, to
which belong the Manifestations of God who, however, have
full knowledge of the entire creation.

The purpose of their Revelations, therefore, is to give life
and meaning to the world of creation, transmitting in a pre-
ordained measure not only the Will of God, but also their
knowledge of the various degrees of reality in a language
understandable to human beings, through Their prayers and
Sacred Writings which thus provide the path of choice for spiritual progress.

In consequence, every phrase, every word and even every
syllable revealed by the Manifestations of God contains infinite
meanings and immense power; to gather even an infinitesimal
part of them it is necessary to come to them with a pure heart,
severed from all attachment: 'A servant is drawn unto Me in
prayer until I answer him, and when I have answered him,
I become the ear wherewith he heareth.'[1] Only a heart that

is completely pure is able to hear His praises and obtain the portion destined for him.

'The purest form of prayer', writes Adib Taherzadeh, ' is one which is freed from desire. Such a prayer will cause the bounties of God to descend upon the soul.'² This is because God desires for His creatures only what is good for them, even when they themselves are not aware of it. So, if we really must ask for something, let us ask for the good-pleasure of God – which means wishing only what God wishes for us, without the least attachment to worldly desires, since with Him alone is the knowledge of all things and the end of all things. Any other desire, even to serve the Cause – however meritorious this may be – will not necessarily lead to salvation if it does not satisfy these requirements:

> I beg of Thee, O my God . . . to ordain that my choice be conformed to Thy choice and my wish to Thy wish, that I may be entirely content with that which Thou didst desire, and be wholly satisfied with what Thou didst destine for me by Thy bounteousness and favour.³

Taherzadeh, with his deep knowledge of the Bahá'í Writings, comments:

> The *Tablet of Ashraf* contains a significant statement concerning the power of prayer when freed from desire. He declares that the outpouring of grace in this day is so great, that should an individual raise his hands in supplication to God and ask for the treasures of earth and heaven, his wish will be granted even before he lowers his hands, provided that he is freed from attachment to all created things. Indeed, the key for attaining the glory lies in the word 'detachment'. From the study of the Writings it becomes

clear that not until man reaches a state of absolute servi-
tude ['*all are His servants*'] wherein he dies to his own self,
and has no desire except what God desires ['*all abide by His
bidding*'], can he ever ascend to such a lofty station. [4]

Who better than Baháʾuʾlláh to tell us what is implied by
detachment?

> Detachment is as the sun; in whatsoever heart it doth shine
> it quencheth the fire of covetousness and self.[5]

And what we need to do to achieve it:

> Thine eye is My trust, suffer not the dust of vain desires
> to becloud its lustre. Thine ear is a sign of My bounty, let
> not the tumult of unseemly motives turn it away from My
> Word that encompasseth all creation. Thine heart is My
> treasury, allow not the treacherous hand of self to rob thee
> of the pearls which I have treasured therein. Thine hand is a
> symbol of my loving-kindness, hinder it not from holding
> fast unto My guarded and hidden Tablets . . . Be light and
> untrammelled as the breeze, that ye may obtain admittance
> into the precincts of My court, My inviolable Sanctuary.[6]

A path that is within the capacity to achieve of every believer,
so as to learn what God asks of us, is well described by Julio
Savi in his book *The Eternal Quest for God*:

> Through prayer . . . a goal is pursued which, as man
> advances in his spiritual growth, rises from an invoca-
> tion aimed at obtaining satisfaction of a material need,
> to a supplication for aid so that a spiritual gift may be
> obtained, to the expression of feelings of contrition for

a past transgression, to feelings of personal helplessness, to an anthem of praise and thanksgiving to God for His abundantly bestowed bounties, to the contemplation of His manifest Beauty in the world of creation and in one's own innermost being.[7]

It is only human to turn toward God, especially (but not only) when we feel overwhelmed by affliction; and both the Báb and Bahá'u'lláh, well aware of human frailty, have revealed special prayers to recite in life's difficult moments. After all, the weak must turn to the Strong in order to obtain His help and His mercy.

But in fact, we should turn to God above all in moments of serenity and joy, when our soul is in the best condition to turn to its Creator in gratitude and unconditional love. In this way a virtuous circle can be established: joy induces prayer and prayer increases our joy.

Nor is this all; there remains the most important aspect, something that goes beyond even the most sublime or sincere praises: the good-pleasure of God! In fact, we read:

Far, far from Thy glory be what mortal man can affirm of Thee, or attribute unto Thee, or the praise with which he can glorify Thee! Whatever duty Thou hast prescribed unto Thy servants of extolling to the utmost Thy majesty and glory is but a token of Thy grace unto them, that they may be enabled to ascend unto the station conferred upon their own inmost being, the station of the knowledge of their own selves.

No one else besides Thee hath, at any time, been able to fathom Thy mystery, or befittingly to extol Thy greatness. Unsearchable and high above the praise of men wilt Thou remain for ever. There is none other God but Thee, the

Inaccessible, the Omnipotent, the Omniscient, the Holy of Holies.[8]

There are some examples of people who rendered notable service to the Cause and yet spiritually their lives ended in tragedy. Let us recall the words of Bahá'u'lláh in the Kitáb-i-Íqán:

How often hath a sinner, at the hour of death, attained to the essence of faith, and quaffing the immortal draught, hath taken his flight unto the Celestial Concourse. And how often hath a devoted believer, at the hour of his soul's ascension, been so changed as to fall into the nethermost fire.[9]

This passage invites reflection on the meaning of detachment from all save God, and consequently the sincerity of our faith. However, writes Taherzadeh,

the most befitting form of prayer is that of praising God. Through it the channels of grace are opened up and He bestows His powers and blessing upon the individual. Turning to God in prayer for the sole purpose of glorifying His Name and extolling His Attributes is the most natural move that man can make towards his Creator.[10]

In a prayer revealed by Bahá'u'lláh Himself we read:

Cause me to taste, O my Lord, the divine sweetness of Thy remembrance and praise . . . Inspire then my soul, O my God, with Thy wondrous remembrance, that I may glorify Thy name. Number me not with them who read Thy words and fail to find Thy hidden gift which, as decreed by Thee, is contained therein, and which quickeneth the souls of Thy creatures and the hearts of Thy servants.[11]

Taherzadeh compares prayer to

> a plant which turns towards the sun. Although the sun
> pours out its energies regardless, yet, by its very nature,
> the tree cannot help but stretch its boughs and branches
> in the direction of the sun. For it to remain insensible to
> the life-giving rays of the sun is a sign that it is dead. To
> use another analogy, we see in nature that a babe cries for
> food and his mother feeds him. But if he does not hunger
> for food, he is not healthy even though the mother may
> feed him by force. This two-way relationship is the basis
> for growth. Similarly, God bestows His boundless favours
> and grace upon His creation, but man must by his own
> volition turn to Him in adoration and praise in order to
> receive them. If he fails to do this, he becomes deprived
> and spiritually starved . . .
>
> The sign of true spiritual life in man is to yearn after
> God and long to adore and glorify Him. The Báb and
> Bahá'u'lláh have shown us the way by revealing most of
> their prayers in praise of God. These prayers evoke in the
> soul feelings of utter self-effacement and absolute poverty,
> while the power of God and His glory become the moti-
> vating influence in guiding and sustaining it throughout
> its life.
>
> The power which can be generated in the heart of the
> believer, when he is freed from all desires and turns to God
> with songs of praise and glorification, is beyond the com-
> prehension of man. Suffice it to say that many heroes of
> the Faith have derived their courage and steadfastness from
> this source.[12]

'Thus far and no further', as it says in Job 38 :11, for God is so
immeasurably far above His creatures that not even the most

exalted praises could ever reach Him except through His will. Have we not just read the verse 'Inspire, then, my soul, O my God . . .', which clearly suggests that a necessary condition for the capacity to glorify God's name is that our soul should be inspired with His 'wondrous remembrance'? If we understand this, we will also come to realize that the act of praising God will nevertheless raise man to the highest station possible to him, which is the knowledge of his own self – since 'he whose sight is illumined with the light of understanding will assuredly detach himself from the world and the vanities thereof'.[13] This is without doubt the greatest 'hidden gift which, as decreed by Thee, is contained therein [His Word], and which quickeneth the souls of Thy creatures and the hearts of Thy servants'.[14]

4

MORE ON PRAYER

In the Baháʾí Faith, as in every revealed religion, every individual is required to give serious attention to his own inner reality, to that essence or emanation of the divine that is his soul, through the development of virtues; but today, in addition, each is required to contribute through his talents to the good of all humankind and to the advancement of a civilization in continual progress. In fact, a key precondition for every accommodation to outer reality is the adjustment of the inner life of the individual, which is itself dependent upon certain essential requirements being fulfilled.

Every individual must first learn to love God. He must learn to have faith in God and in his own soul, which is an emanation of God, just as a ray of the sun is an emanation of that star. He must learn to use a language appropriate to entering into communion with his Creator, and that language is prayer. But above all, he must commit himself to living and acting differently from before. And he must do all this, not from fear of the flames of hell, nor even because he believes that these are good things in themselves, or in order to sublimate or justify difficult realities. He should do these things because he is convinced that they are based on laws as great and as sound as the law of gravity or the principles governing the activity of atoms and stars.

If a friend feels love for another, he wishes to express it;

even if he knows that his friend is aware of his love, he still wants to tell him of it. So, although God knows the desires of every heart, the impulse to pray is natural, it flows from love. Words that are not alive with love are meaningless. If love and desire are not present, it is useless to try to generate them by force. Prayer does not necessarily need to take place in words, still less in a public 'exhibition'; on the contrary, it should be expressed in our thoughts and attitudes when, in the seclusion and intimacy of our own room, we sincerely seek communion with God:

> Whoso reciteth, in the privacy of his chamber, the verses revealed by God, the scattering angels of the Almighty shall scatter abroad the fragrance of the words uttered by his mouth, and shall cause the heart of every righteous man to throb.[1]

Yes, dear friend, we read correctly! the heavenly armies will guarantee that 'the sweetness of thy melody may kindle thine own soul, and attract the hearts of all men', thus descending not only into the depths of your heart (as stated in the next verse of the same passage: 'Though he may, at first, remain unaware of its effect, yet the virtue of the grace vouchsafed unto him must needs sooner or later exercise its influence upon his soul') but, spreading throughout the universe, 'shall cause the heart of every righteous man to throb'.[2] But do we think of this? How can we hope to succeed in truly understanding the significance of this affirmation? Here is the advice given to us by Bahá'u'lláh:

> Immerse yourselves in the ocean of My words, that ye may unravel its secrets, and discover all the pearls of wisdom that lie hid in its depths.[3]

Jesus had already given us the same teachings, phrased in clear and simple terms:

> And when thou prayest, thou shalt not be as the hypocrites are: for they love to pray standing in the synagogues and in the corners of the streets, that they may be seen of men. Verily, I say unto you, they have their reward.
>
> But thou, when thou prayest, enter into thy closet, and when thou has shut thy door, pray to thy Father which is in secret; and thy Father which seeth in secret shall reward thee openly.[4]

If what we seek is approval on the part of other human beings, that will then be our only reward. If, on the other hand, we dare to hope that God, in His infinite mercy, will shower his blessings on us, we must pray with all our inner being.

In this perspective, the brief, most precious prayer revealed by the Báb expresses in its few words all these profound truths.

Is there any Remover of difficulties save God? – signifying that there is no difficulty that God, and He alone, cannot remove so long as it serves our good – is, as previously mentioned, either a supplication in order to obtain a material need or an invocation of help in order to obtain a spiritual gift. Thus it is to Him that we must turn in every situation, since, as 'Abdu'l-Bahá says, 'it is becoming in a weak one to supplicate to the Strong One'.[5]

But immediately afterwards comes the hymn of praise and thanksgiving to God (*Praised be God!*) for the gifts he so copiously pours out, passing then into a state of contemplation of His Beauty compelled by love, for the loving believer cannot do otherwise than name the loved One (*He is God!*)

Only then can the believer realize the full significance of *'all are His servants, and all abide by His bidding'*, and burn with desire to place himself at the service of his Lord and obey His commandments, translating thoughts and intentions into concrete acts, since this is the highest station he is permitted to attain.

So it is not enough to limit ourselves to the simple recitation of a verse, but rather, prayer should follow a dynamic that has been clearly explained by Shoghi Effendi:[6] prayer should be followed by the silence of reflection so that a decision may emerge. Once the decision presents itself as an effective response to our prayer, or as a way of solving a problem – something we can verify only through action, because if doors open and the difficulty gives way to its consequent solution, it is highly probable that the reply we received was the right one and not simply a fruit of our imagination – it is then necessary to feel determined to carry it out to completion; otherwise, a decision that does not become focused in determination to act will remain only a vague wish that leads to a sense of frustration and loss of confidence. We must act in accordance with these words of Bahá'u'lláh:

> The virtues and attributes pertaining unto God are all evident and manifest, and have been mentioned and described in all the heavenly Books. Among them are trustworthiness, truthfulness, purity of heart while communing with God, forbearance, resignation to whatever the Almighty hath decreed, contentment with the things His Will hath provided, patience, nay thankfulness in the midst of tribulation, and complete reliance, in all circumstances, upon Him. These rank, according to the estimate of God, among the highest and most laudable of all acts. All other acts are, and will ever remain, secondary and subordinate unto them.[7]

It is nevertheless indispensable to have faith that the right response to our need will be given so long as we act in conformity with the reply we received – a response that may also differ from our own wishes, because only God knows what is truly good for us. And it is precisely this faith that will unleash in us the strength we need to act, to act untiringly as though the response has already been given, so transforming ourselves like a magnet that attracts further energy.

> O Son of Spirit! Ask not of Me that which We desire not for thee, then be content with what We have ordained for thy sake, for this is that which profiteth thee, if therewith thou dost content thyself.[8]

There are many people who pray, and some who also meditate and arrive at a decision, but who then do not stick to it. Few have the determination to carry out the decision they have taken, and even fewer are those who nourish their faith that the right response will be given to their need.

But in the end, how many will act?

'Greater than the prayer is the spirit thereof,' and even greater than the spirit in which one prays is the act that develops and concretizes it. In the words of Bahá'u'lláh:

> An act, however infinitesimal, is, when viewed in the mirror of the knowledge of God, mightier than a mountain. Every drop proffered in His path is as the sea in that mirror.[9]

If we are spiritually malnourished, feelings of solitude, of being abandoned, frustration and despair can develop and we will no longer able to act in an appropriate way. Spiritual food modifies such feelings:

> The most acceptable prayer is the one offered with the

utmost spirituality and radiance; its prolongation hath not been and is not beloved by God. The more detached and the purer the prayer, the more acceptable is it in the presence of God.[10]

At the dawn of every day he should commune with God, and, with all his soul, persevere in the quest of his Beloved.[11]

Whoso reciteth, in the privacy of his chamber, the verses revealed by God, the scattering angels of the Almighty shall scatter abroad the fragrance of the words uttered by his mouth and shall cause the heart of every righteous man to throb.[12]

Take courage! God never forsakes His children who strive and work and pray![13]

If we telephone a friend to ask advice, we certainly don't hang up before we get a reply. In the same way, we shouldn't get up straight after saying a prayer, but pause to reflect so that we may hear the reply that arises in our heart:

Rely upon God. Trust in Him. Praise Him, and call Him continually to mind. He verily turneth trouble into ease, and sorrow into solace, and toil into utter peace. He verily hath dominion over all things.[14]

There are many occasions when, if we feel overwhelmed by difficulties or anxiety, the best thing to do is to withdraw into the privacy of our room to pray, and to continue as long as we do not feel relief. And we will feel relief only once we are able to get in touch with that inexhaustible fount of energy which is our soul.

In this regard, I recall the following significant incident narrated by Cesare Boni:

I was driving with some friends on the road from Bombay to Delhi. It's called a motorway, but isn't any wider than one of our provincial roads. We were driving nose to tail because the traffic was blocked by a large petrol tanker on the side of the road. As we passed, we asked the driver if he needed help. Shaking his head in typically Indian style, he answered that he didn't need anything, he didn't have any petrol. Looking at the tanker, we asked 'Is it empty?' He replied, 'No, it's full, but we don't know how to connect the big tank to the little tank.'

Although we laughed about it together at the time, in thinking about this incident later it came to my mind that we are like that tank. We have inside us an inexhaustible reserve of strength, of love, of kindness, of joy, of happiness, yet so often we feel spent, tired, arid, sad, unhappy, because we are not constantly connected to this energy. We would just need that contact to solve life's problems, since it is through that contact that our problem of separateness could be overcome. This is work that we must do here and now, because every evolutionary advance, every achievement of consciousness, must be realized here, on this plane of existence, in this life.[15]

A prayer revealed by 'Abdu'l-Bahá helps us make this connection:

O thou who art turning thy face towards God! Close thine eyes to all things else, and open them to realm of the All-Glorious. Ask whatsoever thou wishest of Him alone; seek whatsoever thou seekest from Him alone. With a look He granteth a hundred thousand hopes, with a glance He healeth a hundred thousand incurable ills, with a glimpse He layeth balm on every wound, with a nod He freeth the hearts from the shackles of grief. He doeth as He doeth, and what recourse have we? He carrieth out His Will, He ordaineth what He pleaseth. Then better for thee to bow down thy head in submission, and put thy trust in the All-Merciful Lord.[16]

We only need to try, in order to understand that it really works! – so long, of course, as we are sincere and faithful. In the end, the fundamental thing is to actually repeat the prayer, or a verse, or even a single revealed word, because this can help us to absorb its hidden meaning and the force that is concealed within it:

Blessed the distressed one who seeketh refuge beneath the shadow of My canopy.[17]

Thy name is my healing, O my God, and remembrance of Thee is my remedy. Nearness to Thee is my hope, and love for Thee is my companion. Thy mercy to me is my healing and my succour in both this world and the world to come. Thou, verily, art the All-Bountiful, the All-Knowing, the All-Wise.[18]

And, relevant to our theme:

Is there any Remover of difficulties save God? Say: Praised be God! He is God! All are His servants, and all abide by His bidding.[19]

To which the Báb himself gives the unequivocal response:

Say: God sufficeth all things above all things, and nothing in the heavens or in the earth but God sufficeth. Verily, He is in Himself the Knower, the Sustainer, the Omnipotent.[20]

Or, wishing to be as faithful as possible to what the Báb has revealed, as in the following quotation:

Rid thou thyself of all attachments to aught except God, enrich thyself in God by dispensing with all else besides Him, and recite this prayer:

> Say: God sufficeth all things above all things, and nothing in the heavens or in the earth or in whatever lieth between them but God, thy Lord, sufficeth. Verily, He is in Himself the Knower, the Sustainer, the Omnipotent.

Regard not the all-sufficing power of God as an idle fancy. It is that genuine faith which thou cherishest for the Manifestation of God in every Dispensation. It is such faith which sufficeth above all the things that exist on the earth, whereas no created thing on earth besides faith would suffice thee. If thou are not a believer, the Tree of divine Truth would condemn thee to extinction. If thou art a believer, thy faith shall be sufficient for thee above all things that exist on earth, even thou dost possess nothing.[21]

5

THE PURPOSE OF DIFFICULTIES AND OF OVERCOMING THEM

Is there any Remover of difficulties save God?

This physical world is not an end in itself. It is the workroom for the next world, a place where we can and should develop our 'organs' or spiritual capacities which, according to the Holy Books of all revealed religions, are our virtues, i.e. kindness, respect for our self and for others, love and many others. Virtues are the gifts entrusted to our soul that we should develop and bring to fruition in this life. [1]

One of the conditions needed for their development are difficulties, without which our spiritual potential cannot be realized. As Bahá'u'lláh writes:

> God hath made adversity as a morning dew upon His green pasture, and a wick for His lamp which lighteth earth and heaven. [2]

> My calamity is My providence, outwardly it is fire and vengeance, but inwardly it is light and mercy. [3]

The other ingredients necessary for spiritual growth are our will, and divine guidance. It is up to us to decide to forgive instead of revenging ourselves, to be patient instead of getting angry, to replace feelings of aversion with love. Without the help of divine guidance we would not know how or why we need to reveal the gifts entrusted to our soul.[4]

> Know thou that all men have been created in the nature made by God, the Guardian, the Self-Subsisting. Unto each one hath been prescribed a pre-ordained measure, as decreed in God's mighty and guarded Tablets. All that which ye potentially possess can, however, be manifested only as a result of your own volition.[5]

> These energies with which the Day Star of Divine bounty and Source of heavenly guidance hath endowed the reality of man lie, however, latent within him, even as the flame is hidden within the candle and the rays of light are potentially present in the lamp. The radiance of these energies may be obscured by worldly desires even as the light of the sun can be concealed beneath the dust and dross which cover the mirror. Neither the candle nor the lamp can be lighted through their own unaided efforts, nor can it ever be possible for the mirror to free itself from its dross. It is clear and evident that until a fire is kindled the lamp will never be ignited, and unless the dross is blotted out from the face of the mirror it can never represent the image of the sun nor reflect its light and glory.[6]

The interaction between these three conditions – difficulties, will and divine guidance – enables us to contribute to the well-being of the whole human race and, at the same time, enables us, at the point of our physical death, to move to the next world.[7]

Tests and difficulties often bring with them pain and sadness, and so it's natural that man seeks to avoid them. And

certainly we are not asked to bring useless suffering on ourselves: the God of love who created us wishes for us well-being
and happiness, but only He knows the road we must travel in
order to obtain true happiness.

> I swear by My life! Nothing save that which profiteth them
> can befall My loved ones. To this testifieth the Pen of God,
> the most Powerful, the All-Glorious, the Best Beloved . . .
> Let not the happenings of the world sadden you. I swear
> by God! The sea of joy yearneth to attain your presence,
> for every good thing hath been created for you, and will,
> according to the needs of the times, be revealed unto you.[8]

On this road, we sometimes find obstacles blocking our path
that we must overcome with courage and faith. Often, we are
unable to see anything positive in a seemingly negative situation, despite the fact that life has often taught us that events
we considered painful, terrible, unbearable, have subsequently
revealed to us doors that open to important changes in our
lives, to new happiness, to solutions to problems we had
considered unsolvable. As Alessandro Manzoni writes in *The
Betrothed*, God 'never disturbs the joy of His children, but to
prepare them for one more certain and durable.'[9]

   Therefore, when the bitter cup is at our lips, we must drink
it down without delay, because it is the medicine that will help
us heal our spiritual ills: 'When a man suffers, he ought not to
say: "That's bad! That's bad!" Nothing that God imposes on
man is bad. But it is all right to say: "That's bitter!" For among
medicines there are some that are made with bitter herbs.'[10]
And Bahá'u'lláh writes:

> Happy the days that have been consecrated to the remem-
> brance of God, and blessed the hours which have been

spent in praise of Him Who is the All-Wise . . . Lament not in your hours of trial, neither rejoice therein; seek ye the Middle Way which is the remembrance of Me in your afflictions and reflection over that which may befall you in future. Thus informeth you He Who is the Omniscient, He Who is aware.[11]

To succeed in accepting pain and suffering, it is thus necessary to have an adequate understanding of their purpose – that is, to know why one is suffering, since such knowledge will help us to see this suffering in the wider context of our existence, both present and future. 'Abdu'l-Bahá writes:

When the winds blow severely, rains fall fiercely, the light-ning flashes, the thunder roars, the bolt descends and storms of trial become severe, grieve not; for after this storm, verily, the divine spring will arrive, the hills and fields will become verdant, the expanses of grain will joy-fully wave, the earth will become covered with blossoms, the trees will be clothed with green garments and adorned with blossoms and fruits . . . These favours are results of those storms and hurricanes.[12]

The people we admire most and are attracted to, who instill in us a sense of security, are often those who have suffered most, because suffering often leads to compassion, sensitivity and concern for the needs of others. When we are struck by some adversity that causes pain, we first of all feel vulnerable and in need of help, but little by little it also makes us stronger, to the point where we are able to forget our own suffering in order to help others in pain. This is a virtuous circle that helps to give us more strength, more desire to serve, more awareness of others' needs, and more humility. In the words of Bahá'u'lláh:

Now is the time to cheer and refresh the down-cast through the invigorating breeze of love and fellowship, and the living waters of friendliness and charity . . .

The whole duty of man in this Day is to attain that share of the flood of grace which God poureth forth for him. Let none, therefore, consider the largeness or smallness of the receptacle. The portion of some might lie in the palm of a man's hand, the portion of others might fill a cup, and of others even a gallon-measure.[13]

Sometimes we find ourselves in a situation that might be likened to a bird that, although ready to fly, is too afraid to leave the nest until its parents push it out.

Our nest is the material world; detaching ourselves from it creates in us a sense of anxiety – but we have to do it if we want to fly. The Manifestations of God lovingly push us out of our nest. Only in this way can we, like the bird overcoming the fear of launching itself, rise to heights previously unimaginable when we were safe in our nest; and the higher we fly, the more intense will be the exhilaration we experience, to the point where we miss the nest less and less and have no desire to return to it.

Renouncing the things of this world is a sacrifice that necessarily brings suffering; suffering is thus a vital and indispensable characteristic of life and, therefore, is impossible to avoid.

All calamities and afflictions have been created for man so that he may spurn this mortal world – a world to which he is much attached, When he experienceth severe trials and hardships, then his nature will recoil and he will desire the eternal realm – a realm which is sanctified from all afflictions and calamities. Such is the case with the man who is wise.[14]

In fact, the Báb's prayer says: 'Is there any Remover of difficulties save God?' because, even if we are called upon to act intelligently and responsibly, only God knows what is for our good; He alone 'sufficeth all things above all things, and nothing in the heavens or in the earth but God sufficeth', as the Báb also teaches us in another prayer we all know.

There is a proverb that goes: 'A million flowers bloom every day with no effort on God's part!' Let us learn to find joy in an inescapable process that will help us to emerge, to come into the light: birth is not pain, it is life; nor is death pain – it too is life, because it causes us to emerge in a different world.

But unfortunately, tests and difficulties – above all in the Western world – are experienced with resentment. Instead of trying to understand them, we seek every possible means of ignoring them, to the point of recourse to drugs or alcohol. But in so doing, moral strength is lost, as well as the capacity to courageously confront life's challenges. In the West we have become accustomed to wanting everything to come easily. We think we only need press a button or take a pill, to the point where, as someone says, 'Death doesn't exist in the West' – and in fact death and suffering have become taboo, even though they are an integral part of life. We try to exorcize them by refusing to talk about them or call them by name: so that the plague became 'the disease'; cancer 'an ugly illness' or 'that thing' . . . but life is continual growth, a struggle to keep one's head above water. Nor is it really important whether one is born into a wealthy family or not, even if this may well help to overcome certain difficulties, because life nevertheless brings with it inevitable tests and conflicts.

Of course, there is nothing wrong in trying to constantly better one's own situation, to avoid a paralysing fatalism; on the contrary, man is called upon to 'carry forward an ever-advancing civilization',[15] which clearly implies seeking the well-being of one and all. God, on His part, has created all things for the well-being of His faithful servants, so there is nothing wrong in making use of these things in the right way and in moderation, without – it's worth saying – pinning the hopes of our hearts on material goods. Bahá'u'lláh explains:

> Should a man wish to adorn himself with the ornaments of the earth, to wear its apparels, or partake of the benefits it can bestow, no harm can befall him, if he alloweth nothing whatever to intervene between him and God, for God hath ordained every good thing, whether created in the heavens or in the earth, for such of His servants as truly believe in Him. Eat ye, O people, of the good things which God hath allowed you, and deprive not yourselves from His wondrous bounties. Render thanks and praise unto Him, and be of them that are truly thankful.[16]

The secret lies, not in renouncing the benefits so copiously poured out by the Creator, but in knowing how to value them without becoming uselessly attached to them – for what we own today will not be ours tomorrow, and this can bring us useless suffering. Bahá'u'lláh's words make this clear:

> O friend, the heart is the dwelling of eternal mysteries, make it not the home of fleeting fancies; waste not the treasure of thy precious life in employment with this swiftly-passing world. Thou comest from the world of holiness – bind not thine heart to the earth. Thou art a dweller in the court of nearness – choose not the homeland of the dust.[17]

The world is but a show, vain and empty, a mere nothing, bearing the semblance of reality. Set not your affections upon it . . . Verily I say, the world is like the vapour in a desert, which the thirsty dreameth to be water and striveth after it with all his might, until when he cometh unto it, he findeth it to be mere illusion.[18]

Our growth demands the continual loss of something that seems indispensable to us, but which in fact, in the words of 'Abdu'l-Bahá, is a 'rubbish-heap'.[19]

Man's distinction lieth not in ornaments or wealth, but rather in virtuous behaviour and true understanding.[20]

Men who suffer not, attain no perfection.[21]

Unless one accept suffering, undergo trials and endure vicissitudes he will reap no reward not will he attain success and prosperity.[22]

Through suffering he will attain to an eternal happiness which nothing can take from him.[23]

In the Kitáb-i-Íqán Bahá'u'lláh writes:

. . . from time immemorial even unto eternity the Almighty hath tried, and will continue to try, His servants, so that light may be distinguished from darkness, truth from false-hood, right from wrong, guidance from error, happiness from misery, roses from thorns.[24]

It's not enough to say, 'I believe!' – because He will test our faith.
But if God knows everything, what is the need to test us? He knows perfectly well who has faith and who does not, and He doesn't need to check. He doesn't, but we do! And this for

our own good. First of all because, as 'Abdu'l-Bahá says: 'The mind and spirit of man advance when he is tried by suffering',[25] but above all because we have to prove – not to God who knows everything, but to ourselves – whether our faith is sincere or not: 'So that light may be distinguished from darkness, truth from falsehood, right from wrong, guidance from error, happiness from misery, roses from thorns.'

As in the lobster: the lobster is a soft animal which lives inside a rigid shell. This hard shell does not expand, so how does the lobster grow? Well! With growth, the shell becomes extremely limiting and the lobster ends up feeling pressured and uncomfortable. So, hiding under a rock to protect itself from predators, it gets rid of the old shell and produces a new one. But, in the long run, this shell again becomes uncomfortable. So: back under the rock to change it! And this, over and over again.

The stimulus that enables the lobster to grow arises therefore from a feeling of discomfort. Now, if the lobster had a doctor who at the first sign of trouble gave it Valium or another painkiller to relieve its sufferings, it would never grow because it would not feel the need to break free of its shell. So it is time to understand that difficult moments are also the moments of greatest growth: in fact, we can grow thanks to adversity, if only we are aware of such moments and make good use of them. This is the reason why Bahá'u'lláh invites us not only to be 'generous in prosperity' but also 'thankful in adversity'.

As long as everything goes well, it's easy to believe that we have faith, but it's only when we are subjected to tests that we are able to confirm it, and the harder things become, the more we become aware of our faith, because it is this faith that will be the bulwark that enables us to overcome our tests. 'God hath never burdened any soul beyond its power,' writes Bahá'u'lláh,[26] so we cannot claim even the excuse that we are the victim of an excessively heavy test.

6

TYPES OF AFFLICTION

*A man who fears suffering is already suffering
from what he fears.*
Montaigne

'There are two kinds of affliction in this life,' writes Rúḥíyyih Rabbani in her book *Prescription for Living*:

> one is essential, the other non-essential. Or let us say one is our portion, deliberately given to us for our own good, the other is accidental, produced by a combination of circumstances . . . Life is full of hazards. If you do not look both ways you may be run over crossing the street. You must keep your wits about you and the city must devise ways of controlling the traffic; in this sense there will always be an elimination of suffering in this world, and it is right and proper that people should do all in their power to struggle against and abolish unnecessary suffering and things that cause tragedy, heart-break and illness . . .
>
> But the second kind of suffering, the form that chastens us, forges in the furnace of ordeal the bright sword of our soul, cannot and should not be eliminated.[1]

Perhaps the best lesson can be found in nature. Let's take the example of a butterfly: if you look closely at a chrysalis you can see a small hole at the top. The butterfly pupa must struggle to get its body out through this little hole. Every so often it stops, exhausted, but then renews the struggle – and this for several hours.

We might, through compassion, think that we can help the pupa by making an incision widening the small hole, so that it doesn't have to make too much of an effort to be able to get through and open its wings. But the wings of that butterfly will never open enough to lift it into graceful flight. It will be forced to pass the rest of its life crawling along with a swollen body and shrunken wings. In 'helping' it to emerge from the chrysalis, we will have eliminated the struggle necessary to get through that small hole, provided by mother nature, which pushes the body fluid into the wings so that, once free, they can unfold.

At times, struggle and its ensuing suffering are just what we need in life. Just surfing through with no obstacles will damage us, because we will not be sufficiently strong to take flight.

The logic of divine love is not always easily accessible to human knowledge. There are painful tests which, at the moment they are lived, can seem to be negative but which in fact often provide the stimulus we need to change for the better. A sad event can be positive in terms of psychological growth, providing a balance to a pre-existing lack of harmony we were unaware of. We can only appreciate this point of view once we have processed our pain, once it has become simply part of our existential path – because everything that we leave behind will sooner or later catch up with us and, if it hasn't been dealt with, will continue to cause suffering.[2]

A painful experience can often be revealed as a 'magnifying glass' on our lifestyle, on our connection both to ourselves and to others. Suffering is like working capital: it shouldn't be wasted in becoming depressed, cynical or aggressive; it should be put to use in becoming 'more good'. If, in fact, it is accepted and lived through in a psychologically mature way, it will become a means of growth, a help to understanding oneself and to connection and empathy with others.[3]

Diamonds are formed by the heat and pressure produced within the rock. The most fragrant flowers of the human spirit are frequently those watered by tears. Struggle gives strength, endurance generates greater stamina. We must not run away from life's tests, we must overcome them no matter how hard they are, in order to emerge from them with a stronger character, with greater faith in ourselves and in the Creator Who, like a loving father, educates us and at times punishes us – because He loves us, and because He knows what can be brought forth from each one of us.

Why, then, should we eliminate those factors that cause the best that is in us to emerge, that temper our fibre, that teach us to value happiness at its true worth? How can someone who has never gone hungry appreciate the true value of a crust of bread? (What great wisdom is hidden in the Fast!) If we insist on wanting to live in denial of suffering, we will develop a breed of humans lacking in wisdom and feeling, and without any moral structure.

This is not to say that suffering should be pleasant – we are not asked this much. Jesus Himself was not ashamed to ask if His pain could be avoided when, on the Mount of Olives, he prayed to God: 'O my Father, if it be possible, let this cup pass from me.'[4]

Suffering isn't beautiful, but it is often necessary in creating beauty. We shouldn't consider it to be a virtue in itself, and thus cultivate it through self-mortification or torturing ourselves. But when the bitter cup is raised to our lips and we have no other choice but to drink what it contains – then, as we have already said, we must drink it with energy, determination and courage, aware that while it won't be pleasant, it will strengthen us. Without extremes there are no contrasts, and life becomes monotonous, an interminable grey day – certainly without shadows but also devoid of the glorious light of the sun. All life's components come with their counterpart attached: beauty brings us joy, love bears with it happiness and at times also pain; knowledge provides peace of mind; pain gives us strength, and sorrow can empower our inner self. We need, therefore, to draw from every experience of life the best it has to offer.

Many are the hidden mysteries in God's creation: suffering is undoubtedly one of these. Just think how the vines that are most pruned produce the best grapes. Given the many tests and difficulties undergone in the course of a life, most of the time we don't succeed in understanding their purpose. But while the meaning of suffering cannot be fully appreciated in this world, the effect it produces in an individual can be plainly observed.

In nature, most things are influenced by external forces. For example, a piece of iron is cold and tends to rust if left to itself. But if we chafe it, the friction produces heat and polishes the iron, and if the force is increased it can even become luminous. And it is only this external pressure that brings to light these qualities latent in the iron.

Similarly, there are latent qualities and virtues in human beings which, like precious gems, need to be released from the enormous mass of slag that keeps them prisoner, so that this ballast – which can seem to have become an indispensable part of us – can be discarded even if the process hurts. We must learn to focus on our qualities, not our shortcomings.

But suffering is not so much a symptom as an opportunity:

A man who was afflicted with a terrible disease complained

to Rabbi Israel that his suffering interfered with his learning and praying. The rabbi put his hand on his shoulder
and said: 'How do you know, friend, what is more pleasing
to God, your studying or your suffering?'[5]

Let us consider a pearl, shining by virtue of its intrinsic nature.
If it were covered up, even in silk, its lustre and beauty would
remain hidden. In like manner, human distinction lies not in
games and childish toys, nor in splendid clothes, but in excel-
lent conduct and perseverance in what will befit his station.
Often it is suffering that helps to develop such characteristics,
enabling otherwise hidden qualities to emerge. The pearl mentioned above can serve as an apt example of how a painful
symptom can be transformed into something valuable. The
oyster does not react by eliminating the grain of sand that is
provoking its pain; rather, it incorporates it into its own being,
thus giving back an object of incomparable value – a temple
created from the pain surrounding an impurity, a symbol of
overcoming pain and a clear proof of how painful feelings can
be transformed into something superlatively beautiful. The
thing that caused suffering is now held up to the admiration of
all as something good.

We have to accept the fact that there are things in this life
that we cannot always comprehend, but we can understand a
lot of them, through experience or reason. One of the things
we can comprehend is that a God Who shows Himself at every
instant to be most generous and loving can never submit us
to tests that we are unable to bear and overcome for our own
good, since calamity is outwardly 'fire and vengeance, but
inwardly it is light and mercy'.[6] 'He will never deal unjustly
with anyone, neither will He task a soul beyond its power.'[7]

Since 'adversity is followed by success and rejoicings follow
woe,' we must act so that 'each morn be better than its eve and

each morrow richer than its yesterday,' preserving us 'against idleness and sloth' and enabling us to cling 'unto that which profiteth mankind, whether young or old, whether high or low'.[8]

A beautiful Indian proverb says: 'Be amazed at life every day, as if each was the first, and pray for life as if it were the last.'

We are not alone on this path. It is important to arrive at certainty that God is with us and will help us at every juncture of our lives, so long as we open our hearts, as in the story known as 'Footprints in the Sand':

> One night I dreamed I was walking along the beach with the Lord. Many scenes from my life flashed across the sky. In each scene I noticed footprints in the sand. Sometimes there were two sets of footprints, other times there were one set of footprints.
>
> This bothered me because I noticed that during the low periods of my life, when I was suffering from anguish, sorrow or defeat, I could see only one set of footprints.
>
> So I said to the Lord, 'You promised me, Lord, that if I followed you, you would walk with me always. But I have noticed that during the most trying periods of my life there have only been one set of footprints in the sand. Why, when I needed you most, have you not been there for me?'
>
> The Lord replied: 'The times when you have seen only one set of footprints, is when I carried you.'[9]

God wants us to be strong and victorious, because this is the inheritance He has prepared for us. To become aware to this, we only need to re-read some of the verses of the Báb's Address to the Letters of the Living:

> O My beloved friends! . . . The time is come when naught but the purest motive, supported by deeds of stainless

purity, can ascend to the throne of the Most High and be acceptable unto Him. 'The good word riseth up unto Him, and the righteous deed will cause it to be exalted before Him.'. . . You have been chosen as the repositories of His mystery. It behoves each one of you to manifest the attributes of God, and to exemplify by your deeds and words the signs of His righteousness, His power and glory. The very members of your body must bear witness to the loftiness of your purpose, the integrity of your life, the reality of your faith, and the exalted character of your devotion' . . . 'Ye are even as the fire which in the darkness of the night has been kindled upon the mountain-top. Let your light shine before the eyes of men . . . You are the salt of the earth, but if the salt have lost its savour, wherewith shall it be salted?'[10]

'Knock, and it shall be opened'; so it is written in the Gospels. He will stretch out His Hand to us if we invoke Him, while if we stretch ours towards Him He will take it with strength, as Julio Savi writes in *The Eternal Quest for God*:

Whoever has recognized the traces of God in the universe feels himself no longer as a knowing, feeling and willing creature forsaken, a tiny meaningless atom upon a grain of dust wandering about through unbounded space. The world around is no longer threatening and awesome, unknown and hostile . . . Whoever has found God in the universe feels the joy of being part of a total harmony which may sometimes be incomprehensible in some of its aspects, but which is always fundamentally a friendly reality . . . he feels serene in his heart, as one who can rely upon the support of mighty powers which are at the disposal of anyone who wants to seize them . .

This man does not feel that earthly life is vain: he feels the soundness and the joy of a creative commitment which is bound to yield its fruit of inner growth and which will therefore win its intended, longed-for prize.

Whoever discovers God in the universe discovers a perfect and marvellous order in sensible reality, a subtle, miraculous equilibrium whereby that apparently discordant world appears as an organic unit; thus he understands and feels the necessity both of creating such an ideal order in his own personal microcosm as well, and of attuning his own microcosm to all the microcosms which make up society. Willingly therefore will he shoulder the challenging responsibility of following the standards of inner personal and outer social order . . . in this way he will achieve the development of his own potentialities and – through the creation of a harmonious society – contribute to those of other human beings . . .

Last but not least, a man who has discovered an order and a harmony in both macrocosm and microcosm will be able to harmonize the objective reality of creation with the subjective reality of his experience of his own self and of the cosmos, and thus he will 'live in conscious at-one-ment with the eternal world'.[11] This 'at-one-ment' is the essence of joy: the aesthetic enjoyment of a common origin, of belonging to one and the same order, whose conscious experience is conducive to a deep love, to an attraction founded upon the same divine fatherhood. This joy is identical, whether it comes from the contemplation of the wonders of existence or from the observation and study of the fruits of man's efforts to express through his own means the beauty that has been plentifully lavished upon creation by the bountiful hand of a divine Creator.[12]

In the words of the poet Keats:

> Beauty is truth, truth beauty, – that is all
> Ye know on earth, and all ye need to know.[13]

We need to accept the fact that our soul, although eternal, is bound in this life in the net of circumstances, with all their opportunities and limitations. Consequently we must cherish every possible moment of our life, resting when necessary but always tending in the direction of the divine Light, without letting ourselves lose heart in difficult moments.

'Abdu'l-Bahá perfectly expresses this concept when he encourages us not to indulge in physical rest for its own sake:

> . . . if he sleep, it should not be for pleasure, but to rest the body in order to do better, to speak better, to explain more beautifully, to serve the servants of God and to prove the truths. When he remains awake, he should seek to be attentive, serve the Cause of God and sacrifice his own stations for those of God. When he attains to this station, the confirmations of the Holy Spirit will surely reach him, and man with this power can withstand all who inhabit the earth.[14]

As we proceed towards our goal, it's important to reflect every morning when we awake: 'Thank you, O God, for this splendid day You have given me. Help me, I pray, to keep it thus!' The sun shines always and, even when it rains, we should not forget that this means that the dark clouds will soon disappear and dissolve, while the sun ever remains the same and never fails. It is good to remember this in times of difficulty and loneliness. This state of mind is well expressed in the prayer of the great Sufi Dhu'l-Nun al-Misri (d. 861 AD):

O God, I recognize Thee in the ordeals to which I am sub-jected. Allow Thy satisfaction to be my satisfaction. May I be Thy joy, the joy a father feels for a child. And let me remember Thee with serenity and determination, even when it is hard to say that I love Thee.[15]

Let us close this chapter with this anonymous ancient pearl of wisdom from the Chinese:

A wise old sage was walking in a field covered in snow, when he saw a woman weeping.

'Why do you weep?' he asked her.

'Because I am remembering the past, my youth, the beauty I used to see in the mirror, the men I have loved. God has been cruel to me, because He has given me the remembrance of these things. He knew I would remember the springtime of my life and would weep for it.'

The wise man began to contemplate the snowy field, fixing his gaze on a particular point. In a while the woman stopped crying: 'What are you looking at?' she asked.

'A field of roses,' said the wise man. 'God has been gen-erous to me, because He has given me the remembrance of these things. He knew that in winter I could always remember the spring, and smile.'

7

THE MYSTERY OF SACRIFICE

We usually associate the idea of sacrifice with losing something, with renouncing something, with even some kind of mortification which has long ago lost its significance and purpose. And so we experience it as a terrible thing, some kind of punishment we have to undergo. But the opposite could in fact be true: where sacrifice is the fulfilment of a sacred act, that is, an act that gives value and meaning to us and to our life.

But who better than 'Abdu'l-Bahá to come to our aid in clarifying this idea? Let us see, then, what he said about the mystery of sacrifice – for example during His visit to the United States and Canada. And so I propose here an extract from *The Promulgation of Universal Peace*, the collection of talks given by 'Abdu'l-Bahá during that historic journey.

This evening I wish to speak to you concerning the mystery of sacrifice. There are two kinds of sacrifice: the physical and the spiritual . . .

In order to understand the reality of sacrifice let us consider the crucifixion and death of Jesus Christ. It is true that He sacrificed Himself for our sake. What is the meaning of this? When Christ appeared, He knew that He must proclaim Himself in opposition to all the nations and peoples of the earth . . . He realized that His blood would be shed and His body rent by violence. Notwithstanding

His knowledge of what would befall Him, He arose to proclaim His message . . . He accepted every calamity and suffering in order to guide men to the truth. Had He desired to save His own life, and were He without wish to offer Himself in sacrifice, He would not have been able to guide a single soul. There was no doubt that His blessed blood would be shed and His body broken. Nevertheless, that Holy Soul accepted calamity and death in His love for mankind. This is one of the meanings of sacrifice.[1]

In this talk to a Christian audience, 'Abdu'l-Bahá refers specifically to the crucifixion of Christ. But, as he did on other occasions, he could have give the example of any other Manifestation of God. Since our reflections here concern one of the prayers revealed by the Báb, let us take His example, particularly in light of the astounding similarity between the events of His life and the life of Jesus. Both were young (Jesus was 30, the Báb 25 years old) when They declared Their missions, which were each destined to be brief (six years for the Báb, three for Jesus) and culminated in their martyrdom (the crucifixion of Christ and the execution of the Báb by a regiment of 750 guns) in the company of a pure soul (the good thief in the case of Jesus and Anís in that of the Báb). Before being martyred, both openly proclaimed Their mission before the religious authorities, and took leave of Their disciples with exactly the same admonition: 'You are the salt of the earth, but if the salt has lost its savour, wherewith shall it be salted?'

'Abdu'l-Bahá continues:

As to the second meaning: He said, 'I am the living bread which came down from heaven.' It was not the body of Christ which came from heaven. His body came from the womb of Mary, but the Christly perfections descended from heaven; the reality of Christ came down from heaven. The Spirit of Christ and not the body descended from heaven. The body of Christ was but human. There could be no question that the physical body was born from the womb of Mary. But the reality of Christ, the Spirit of Christ, the perfections of Christ all came from heaven. Consequently, by saying He was the bread which came from heaven He meant that the perfections which He showed forth were divine perfections, that the blessings within Him were heavenly gifts and bestowals, that His light was the light of Reality. He said, 'If any man eat of this bread, he shall live for ever.' That is to say, whosoever assimilates these divine perfections which are within me will never die; whosoever has a share and partakes of these heavenly bounties I embody will find eternal life; he who takes unto himself these divine lights shall find everlasting life. How manifest the meaning is! How evident! For the soul which acquires divine perfections and seeks heavenly illumination from the teachings of Christ will undoubtedly live eternally. This is also one of the mysteries of sacrifice . . .

As to the third meaning of sacrifice, it is this: If you plant a seed in the ground, a tree will become manifest from that seed. The seed sacrifices itself to the tree that will come from it. The seed is outwardly lost, destroyed; but the same seed which is sacrificed will be absorbed and embodied in the tree, its blossoms, fruit and branches. If the identity of that seed had not been sacrificed to the tree which became manifest from it, no branches, blossoms or fruits would have been forthcoming. Christ outwardly disappeared . . . but the bounties, divine qualities and perfections of Christ became manifest in the Christian community which Christ founded through sacrificing Himself . . . Christ, like unto the seed, sacrificed Himself for the tree of Christianity.

Therefore, His perfections, bounties, favours, lights and graces became manifest in the Christian community, for the coming of which He sacrificed Himself.

As to the fourth significance of sacrifice: It is the principle that a reality sacrifices its own characteristics. Man must sever himself from the influences of the world of matter, from the world of nature and its laws; for the material world is the world of corruption and death. It is the world of evil and darkness, of animalism and ferocity, bloodthirstiness, ambition and avarice, of self-worship, egotism and passion; it is the world of nature. Man must strip himself of all these imperfections, must sacrifice these tendencies which are peculiar to the outer and material world of existence.

On the other hand, man must acquire heavenly qualities and attain divine attributes. He must become the image and likeness of God. He must seek the bounty of the eternal, become the manifestor of the love of God, the light of guidance, the tree of life and the depository of the bounties of God. That is to say, man must sacrifice the qualities and attributes of the world of nature for the qualities and attributes of the world of God. For instance, consider the substance we call iron. Observe its qualities; it is solid, black, cold. These are the characteristics of iron. When the same iron absorbs heat from the fire, it sacrifices its attribute of solidity for the attribute of fluidity. It sacrifices its attribute of darkness for the attribute of light, which is a quality of the fire. It sacrifices its attribute of coldness to the quality of heat which the fire possesses . . .

Likewise, man, when separated and severed from the attributes of the world of nature, sacrifices the qualities and exigencies of that mortal realm and manifests the perfections of the Kingdom . . .

Every man trained through the teachings of God and illumined by the light of His guidance, who becomes a believer in God and His signs and is enkindled with the fire of the love of God, sacrifices the imperfections of nature for the sake of divine perfections. Consequently, every perfect person, every illumined, heavenly individual stands in the station of sacrifice. It is my hope that through the assistance and providence of God and through the bounties of the Kingdom of Abhá you may be entirely severed from the imperfections of the world of nature, purified from selfish, human desires, receiving life from the Kingdom of Abhá and attaining heavenly graces.[2]

In Chapter 3 on the power and purpose of prayer, we said that God desires for His creatures what is good for them. 'Abdu'l-Bahá tells us that Christ, in common with other Manifestations of God, 'accepted calamity and death in His love for mankind'. It's reasonable to suppose that His sacrifice was made so that man could know happiness.

But if we stop to reflect, we will realize that the prayers and Writings of the Faith do not explicitly tell us that man is born primarily to be happy, so much as to love and serve God. At the start of this book we hazarded the suggestion of a parallel between the Báb's prayer, 'Is there any Remover of difficulties . . . ' and the short Obligatory Prayer revealed by Bahá'u'lláh, where the believer affirms: 'I bear witness, I my God, that Thou hast created me to know Thee and to worship Thee . . .'. To worship God implies loving and serving Him; this is inherent in the dynamic of prayer. And on this path, Bahá'u'lláh tells us, it is not we who put God to the test but God who tests us; this is the path of sacrifice that permits us to 'taste' of His presence and thus becomes a source of cosmic joy which nothing can undermine.

The end result is closely linked to the path we have trodden, with all its difficulties. The rainbow appears after the storm: and the more violent the storm, the more resplendent and reassuring is the rainbow. Have you ever asked yourself why one of the most interesting childhood games is kite-flying? The strong contrary winds that are necessary for the kite to take flight sometimes also destroy it, to the consternation of the child. But only in rising to this challenge will the child at last succeed in getting the kite to fly – and only then will his heart and spirit feel the wonderful sense of freedom as he sees it flying higher and higher in the sky.

INTERMEZZO

Cultivate three things: goodness, wisdom and friendship.
Seek three things: truth, philosophy and understanding.
Love three things: good manners, value and service.
Govern three things: character, language and conduct.
Enjoy three things: friendliness, cheerfulness and decency.
Defend three things: honour, friends and the weak.
Admire three things: talent, dignity and grace.
Exclude three things: ignorance, offense and envy.
Fight three things: the lie, hate and slander.
Preserve three things: health, reputation and good humour . . .[1]

GOD LOVES LAUGHTER

In the past, the saying 'If God wishes' or 'God willing', was viewed not as a kind of passive fatalism, but rather a sign of trust in Providence, without avoiding responsibility. We are asked to act intelligently, given that the mind is the greatest gift of God to man, and 'in the estimation of men of wisdom keenness of understanding is due to keenness of vision'.[2] If God were always to act according to our wishes or how we think he should, he would no longer be the Omnipotent, the Omniscient, but simply an extension of man.

The shield that protects us from our own imagination is faith – that is, that reassuring certitude during life's tests and against the fear of death (it is no coincidence that some find their faith again only at the point of death). Life is tragic, given inevitable illness, failure and disappointment, and it invariably culminates in what is often considered the final tragedy: death itself. But in the very essence of life and being lies a profound joy; this, perhaps, is what inspired Woody Allen to say: 'Life is full of misery, loneliness, and suffering – and it's all over much too soon.'

But still, man is not born primarily for happiness, but to love and serve God in this life ('*all are His servants*'). Happiness is a consequence. It is not for us to put God to the test (our egocentricity leads us to imagine that God is at our beck and call, so that we often run to Him as a child runs to its parents when it falls down and hurts its knee), but it is God Who tests us. It is only from this viewpoint that religion can become a source of cosmic joy, because it can evoke in the human heart 'the virtues and attributes pertaining unto God', and it is only in the human heart that these virtues, these attributes 'are all evident and manifest'.[3]

These virtues can make each human being a unique child of God, the generous Father Who desires him to be 'a happy and joyful being' through his sincere readiness 'to lay all his affairs in His hand'.[4] This allows him to arrive at the thought, as did Victor Hugo mourning the death of his beloved daughter, that perhaps human sorrows are an element in God's hidden purpose, are useful in ways we cannot understand, but know by faith to be positive.[5] Bahá'u'lláh Himself confirms:

> Know ye that trials and tribulations have, from time imme-morial, been the lot of the chosen Ones of God and His beloved, and such of His servants as are detached from all else but Him . . . Such is God's method carried into effect of old, and such will it remain in the future. Blessed are the steadfastly enduring, they that are patient under ills and hardships, who lament not over anything that befalleth them, and who tread the path of resignation.[6]

Thus we can say, with Job in the Bible, when we lose something or someone dear to us: 'The Lord giveth, the Lord hath taken away, blessed be the name of the Lord!' (*'Praised be God!'*).

As we have seen, there are two kinds of tests: those that life brings to every one of us and which each individual must there-fore face with faith and courage, conscious that they serve his development; and those that may be called 'accidental', from the fact that we live in a contingent world subject to natural laws which, although perfect in themselves, can sometimes bring severe difficulties upon us.

Our marvellous planet, in common with the whole universe of which it is a part, has been and continues to be changed by catastrophic events; if on one hand these have created wide oceans, majestic mountain chains and fertile plains together with their myriad forms of life, on the other hand they have also provoked untold disasters generating immense suffering, struggle and even the extinction of forms of life they had earlier contributed to creating.

We may be overcome by fear and legitimate doubt in the bounty of creation and its Maker, or even in His existence. We may resign ourselves to merely surviving, in expectation of our inevitable sad fate – or we can hold our head above the waves, above the breakers of life, and allow ourselves to be overwhelmed in wonder at the beauty that is being born in our heart, a beauty that is a path to the sacred.

Even if it is God alone Who can remove difficulties, that same God does not wish us to sit weeping over them; rather, He asks us to struggle and confront the vicissitudes of life with humour, because 'God loves laughter'.[7] God loves those who know how to laugh, who can see the irony in a situation. A sense of humour is among the most precious qualities of the human spirit; it is a purely human virtue, like knowledge or compassion.

We recall that Job was a good man, but God made him suffer in order to test his faith. He took away everything he had: house, fortune, family, health, in order to test his faith . . . 'But', it might occur to us, 'wasn't God exaggerating a bit?'

If this seems irreverent, let's remember that God loves laughter, because it is those who are pure in heart who are able to laugh. We have to approach the absolute with a sense of irony: a Hebrew saint in a Hasidic story could even allow himself to say, 'I laugh at God because I see how the world is made'; he was a saint despite – and above all because of – his sense of irony, inseparable from his religious feeling.

Irony is, in fact, consciousness of the relativity of everything human; laughter – that laughter where so much sorrow and so much love for the human condition resounds – is the chemical agent that dissolves the smoke of false secrets, that demystifies human stupidity disguised as mystery.

Faith implies complete confidence in God, a life so infused with His presence as to permit even a little irreverence and familiarity, as between children and parents who love each other; a sense that God is indissolubly fused into one's being, to the point where this constitutes one's vitality, strength and feeling of being rooted in existence, a feeling often seduced away by the melancholy or depression that empties reality of significance and pleasure.[8]

This feeling is a continual source of comfort and an inexhaustible fount of patience when we are confronted by life's challenges. Such a feeling compassionately mitigates that sense of responsibility that can so easily becoming paralysing, and that guarantees that we may well take ourselves and others too seriously; it leads us to a vision of life where humour has its proper place,[9] with its capacity to prevent tragedy. By laughing in the face of a tragic reality we do not, of course, change it, but we transform our perception of it

The chief benefit of a sense of humour, as with wit and irony, is the effect it has on our inner life, since it allows us to distance ourselves clearly from the circumstances. It is not a case of being superficial; on the contrary, many spiritual traditions have found humorous responses to existential problems. In the final chapter we will explore, from various traditions, some of these little stories that demonstrate the profound truth of a smile.

In addition, God asks us even to 'wrestle' with Him. The heroic symbol of this struggle is the case of Jacob, who wrestled with the angle and conquered him, and *because of this* God blessed him![10]

Irony and struggle! What could be more revolutionary – writes Alessandro Bausani – more removed from some kinds of 'religion' or drawing-room religiosity?[11]

But why such struggle? God permits it, in order for man to better understand the idea that he is made in the image of God. God voluntarily concedes this struggle to man, but in order to suggest something to him – that is, that the Object of our adoration is far removed from the limitations of our understanding.

It is useless to try understand the significance of God's command in ever more refined arguments. He is truly wise who considers such things simply as a compass indicating the divine nucleus that is in man, given that 'he who has known himself has known God'. But whoever thinks he has found the answer is in trouble. To know oneself is the most difficult and risky enterprise; to bring to light everything that is in us is a vain pretension. This, however, is not a curse, rather a blessing that stems from our unconscious.[12] After all, as James Joyce has his characters say, we are 'darkness shining in the brightness'.[13] Unfortunately, as someone else has said, most of the time we limit ourselves to dwelling on the wise man's finger pointing at the moon.

Only someone who knows himself, who knows how to *be* himself, can fear a little less the reprimand of the Lord that Rabbi Zusya felt threatened by. On the point of death, he said, 'In the coming world, they will not ask me: "Why were you not Moses?" They will ask me: "Why were you not Zusya?"'[14]

It has been said that 'praise precedes faith'.[15] Failure to praise God will block one's faith. It's no coincidence that in the prayer of the Báb the phrase 'Praised be God!' precedes the declaration 'He is God!'

The development of faith towards its maturity includes uncertainty, doubt, anxiety and conflict – all necessary phases in the 'growth crises' of 'normal' individuals. Sometimes when we find ourselves in difficulties we panic and get into a 'crisis'. Then, perhaps, is the moment to consider that the word 'crisis' can have other meanings. In Greek, for example, the language from which our word is derived, it means 'judgement', while in Chinese it also means 'opportunity'. That difficulties are also opportunities has already been stated in an earlier chapter, but it's always useful to say it again. In fact, the Manifestions of God appear precisely when humanity is spiritually sick – in 'crisis' – to teach people to heal themselves and others, to become instruments of the 'new creation', to carry forward an ever-advancing civilization and to carry out (in the words of Jesus Christ), works greater than those done by Himself.

The prevailing forces of fear and pessimism pervading society must be challenged by a growing consciousness of wonder and of blessing – for the path of wonder and awe is the beginning of understanding, of true knowledge. The world today needs understanding, that is, knowledge permeated by wisdom, for knowledge alone can even be dangerous.

The prophetic tradition is a tradition of joy and blessing in the midst of pain, of hope in the midst of injustice. It is we ourselves who, in separating joy from spirituality, increase mistrust, injustice and suffering. No-one comes into the world in sin, but in joy and benediction. As creatures who carry within ourselves the image of God, every one of us is surrounded from the beginning by God's love.

But, as Bahá'u'lláh also writes: 'If thou lovest Me not, My love can in no wise reach thee. Know this, O servant.'[16] How often do we place a veil between ourselves and God, hiding His image that is within us! This is the main cause of all our difficulties.

The focal point is recognition of the Manifestation of God: 'I bear witness, O my God, that Thou hast created me to know Thee and to worship Thee'.[17] The 'chosen people' of the Abhá Kingdom are those who have recognized in Bahá'u'lláh the Manifestation of God for our time, but fundamentally, it is humility that is important ('humility, like darkness, reveals the heavenly lights')[18] – a humility that protects us from pride, which will otherwise certainly lead to tests and difficulties.

> From amongst all mankind hath He chosen you, and your eyes have been opened to the light of guidance and your ears attuned to the music of the Company above; and blessed by abounding grace, your hearts and souls have been born into new life. Thank ye and praise ye God that the hand of infinite bestowals hath set upon your heads this gem-studded crown, this crown whose lustrous jewels will forever flash and sparkle down all the reaches of time.[19]

To be invested with such a privilege, to be immersed in the love of God, is a raging fire that can burn away everything – even the believer himself, unless he assumes his part of responsibility to place himself in God's service and unless he is sincere in his faith. ('Be thou of the people of hell-fire, but be not a hypocrite,' writes Bahá'u'lláh.[20] It is better to be sincere in one's doubts than hypocritical in one's faith.)

The above passage in fact continues as follows:

> To thank Him for this, make ye a mighty effort, and choose for yourselves a noble goal. Through the power of faith, obey ye the teachings of God, and let all your actions conform to His laws.

As Shoghi Effendi emphasizes:

They cannot be the chosen people of God, – the ones who have received the bounty of accepting Him . . . and do nothing about it.[21]

And he also writes:

They should not content themselves merely with relative distinction and excellence. Rather they should fix their gaze upon nobler heights by setting the counsels and exhortations of the Pen of Glory as their supreme goal. Then it will be readily realized how numerous are the stages that still remain to be traversed and how far off the desired goal lies – a goal which is none other than exemplifying heavenly morals and virtues.[22]

These are just a few reflections that may perhaps help us in the second part of this book to ponder further on what we have read in the first part, and at the same time prepare us for the next chapters.

These themes are so deep that they can be neither communicated nor appreciated in words alone. They are among those truths that only the heart, a heart 'illuminated' or that 'knows' through experience, can transmit to another heart. I have no claim to such depth, but hope, starting from a level accessible to anyone, to have been sufficiently clear and simple and to be able to continue in the same vein. As the philosopher Nietzsche has written:

Those who know they are deep strive for clarity. Those who would like to seem deep to the crowd strive for obscurity. For the crowd takes everything whose ground it cannot see to be deep: it is so timid and so reluctant to go into the water.[23]

PART TWO

'PRAISED BE GOD! HE IS GOD! ALL ARE HIS SERVANTS AND ALL ABIDE BY HIS BIDDING!'

8

TO PRAISE GOD

Praised be God!

We can now understand why the Báb's prayer continues with
the words: 'Praised be God! He is God!' A careful reading of
these verses can raise no other desire in one's heart than to seek
the tranquillity of one's own room in order to lift high one's
praise to God, and to allow every cell in one's body to vibrate
in perfect harmony with such praise. We can experience this
feeling not only in the intimate setting of our own room, but
also when we find ourselves in one of those places where nature
itself speaks to us of the bounty of the Creator and steals our
hearts away with its beauty.

How can one remain indifferent to the poetic words
gleaned from the prayers of Bahá'u'lláh, such as the following
examples?

> Every time I lift up mine eyes unto Thy heaven, I call to
> mind Thy highness and Thy loftiness, and Thine incompa-
> rable glory and greatness; and every time I turn my gaze to
> Thine earth, I am made to recognize the evidences of Thy
> power and the tokens of Thy bounty. And when I behold
> the sea, I find that it speaketh to me of Thy majesty, and
> of the potency of Thy might, and of Thy sovereignty and
> Thy grandeur. And at whatever time I contemplate the

mountains, I am led to discover the ensigns of Thy victory and the standards of Thine omnipotence.

. . . I am so inflamed by my love for Thee, and so inebriated with the wine of Thy oneness, that I can hear from the whisper of the winds the sound of Thy glorification and praise, and can recognize in the murmur of the waters the voice that proclaimeth Thy virtues and Thine attributes, and can apprehend from the rustling of the leaves the mysteries that have been irrevocably ordained by Thee in Thy realm.[1]

I testify that no thought of Thee, howsoever wondrous, can ever ascend into the heaven of Thy knowledge, and no praise of Thee, no matter how transcendent, can soar up to the atmosphere of Thy wisdom . . .

. . . I am persuaded of my powerlessness to describe and extol Thee in a manner that becometh the greatness of Thy glory and the excellence of Thy majesty.[2]

Though I recognize and firmly believe that no description which any except Thyself can give of Thee can beseem Thy grandeur, and that no glory ascribed to Thee by any save Thyself can ever ascend into the atmosphere of Thy presence, yet were I to hold my peace, and cease to glorify Thee and to recount Thy wondrous glory, my heart would be consumed, and my soul would melt away.

My remembrance of Thee, O my God, quencheth my thirst, and quieteth my heart. My soul delighteth in its communion with Thee . . . and my heart panteth after Thee even as one sore athirst panteth after the living waters of Thy bounty . . .[3]

But, as 'Abdu'l-Bahá reminds us, we must translate thought

into action, so that the praise of God can result in what Bahá'u'lláh describes in the following Tablet:

> We desire to mention him who hath set his face towards Us and to let him once again drink deep from the life-giving waters of Our gracious Providence that he may be enabled to draw nigh unto My Horizon, be adorned with Mine attributes, soar in Mine atmosphere, be confirmed in that which will cause the sanctity of My Cause to be manifested amongst My people and to celebrate My praise in a manner that will cause every hesitating soul to hasten, every motionless creature to wing its flight, every chilled heart to be stirred with life and every dejected spirit to surge with delight.[4]

In order for this translating of thought into action to be successful, faith and consistency are indispensable. In other words, if I pray for rain, I should go out with my umbrella! And so it may be useful to recall the following story (perhaps apocryphal) told about 'Abdu'l-Bahá by one of the early believers:

One day, when their land was suffering from a long-standing drought, some people came to 'Abdu'l-Bahá to ask Him, when He next prayed, to beg God for a little reviving rain. And lo and behold, there was a flood! So the same people came back to thank 'Abdu'l-Bahá. But He said they should thank, not Him, but their young friend who since their first visit had been going around with his umbrella in spite of the burning sun.

9

OVERCOMING DIFFICULTIES

Ci sono delusioni che pesano
sul cuore come macigni,
andare avanti diventa difficile.
Ma tu ricorda sempre che,
qualunque cosa accada
potranno frantumare un sogno
ma non la tua capacità di rialzarti
e credere che tu meriti molto di più.
Combatti e affronta la delusione
con quella luce che arriva
dritta dritta da dentro di te.

Stephen Littleword[1]

(*There are disappointments that weigh like boulders on the heart; to go ahead becomes difficult. But always remember that anything can crush a dream, but not your ability to get up again and believe you deserve a lot more. Fight, and face the disappointment with the light that comes from directly inside you.*)

When the Báb was journeying to Mecca on pilgrimage, the small boat he and his companions were travelling on was buffeted by violent storms for several days. The sea was so high that all the passengers feared for their lives – only the Báb remained perfectly calm. Why? Because He had placed everything in God's hands! Who, more than the Báb, could be certain that the only 'Remover of difficulties' is God? And so, in complete faith the Báb continued to prepare Himself spiritually for pilgrimage, raising praises to God (*Praised be God! He is God!*).

It is necessary to have faith in the grace of God, even when such grace is not shown in the way we would like it to be. As we have seen in an earlier chapter, Bahá'u'lláh writes:

Ask not of Me that which We desire not for thee, then be content with what We have ordained for thy sake, for this is that which profiteth thee, if therewith thou dost content thyself.[2]

And, addressing God, he counsels us:

We should wish only what Thou has wished for us. In Thee is the knowledge of all things, and with Thee is the issue of all things. Thou art, verily, the Truth, the Knower of things unseen.[3]

The difficulty lies precisely in the fact that, while we expect the grace of God to manifest itself in the way we want, God knows what we truly need – and that is what He gives us in his abounding mercy. When we don't succeed in understanding this truth we become impatient and feel unsatisfied, and this may lead us to stop praising God, in the belief that He is not looking after us. If we get bogged down in these negative thoughts rather than being content with the will of God, they will result in a kind of paralysis. The only sure way out of this is, on the one hand, to give up our own desires, and on the other, to act. To act in the conviction that even if the result is the opposite of what we originally wanted, we will in fact have won a victory.

Our impatience can at first make such a victory seem like defeat, but if we persevere, as impatience is quieted and gives way to inner peaceful integrity, the heart will be moved at last to confess to itself that to be content with the will of God is worthwhile – further, that it is the only good worth seeking, that it is the only one that it is blessed to possess.

It is the heart that experiences divine solace, the deepest and most lasting of all solace. Then, little by little, the human heart will become ever more 'intemperate' – but in a good sense, that is, increasingly longing, increasingly desiring the assurance of mercy. Thus, the more we turn our heart to God, the greater will be the solace we draw from Him, and all fear will vanish away. Through this, our full confidence that only God can remove difficulties is tested and thus acquired – if in life's difficult moments, instead of pitying ourselves, complaining or being afraid, we raise our praises to God and carry out acts of faith, while from the depths of our heart we sincerely repeat 'He is God!', unconditionally submitting our own will to the will of God.

Our only weapon is prayer: a prayer that will have the effect described by Bahá'u'lláh in *The Seven Valleys*:

> Whensoever the light of Manifestation of the King of Oneness settleth upon the throne of the heart and soul, His shining becometh visible in every limb and member.[4]

As mentioned earlier, when we become detached from all else but God we will be predisposed to listening to His Word with His own ears:

> 'A servant is drawn unto Me in prayer until I answer him;

and when I have answered him, I become the ear wherewith he heareth . . .' For thus the Master of the house hath appeared within His home, and all the pillars of the dwelling are ashine with His light. And the action and the effect of the light are from the Light-Giver; so it is that all move through Him and arise by His will.[5]

And although we may not know what will happen after the last word of our prayer – God willing – has risen to heaven, nothing should weaken our certitude that, whatever happens will be for the best:

A lover feareth nothing and no harm can come nigh him . . .[6]

Love is a light that never dwelleth in a heart possessed by fear.[7]

Both Bahá'u'lláh and 'Abdu'l-Bahá exhort us to dedicate more of our time to prayer and meditation. In the words of Bahá'u'lláh:

Happy the days that have been consecrated to the remembrance of God, and blessed the hours which have been spent in praise of Him Who is the All-Wise.[8]

Lament not in your hours of trial, neither rejoice therein; seek ye the Middle Way which is the remembrance of Me in your afflictions and reflection over that which may befall you in future. Thus informeth you He Who is the Omniscient, He Who is aware.[9]

When we pray and meditate, we create a safe environment for

ourselves *and within ourselves*, an environment that neutral-
izes those negative thoughts which feed our anxieties and fears
that stem from difficult situations and stressful events. When
we feel overcome by fear and anxiety, that is the moment to
dedicate more time to prayer and meditation, to draw comfort
from them and receive the right answer to our problems. And
then to act in consequence.

> Were men to discover the motivating purpose of God's
> Revelation, they would assuredly cast away their fears, and,
> with hearts filled with gratitude, rejoice with exceeding
> gladness.[10]

Patience is an essential help in overcoming difficulties. Our
capacity to be patient in difficulties is determined by our capacity to have confidence that in the end we will be relieved. And
thus patience and faith may be considered to be interdepend-
ent. The more our faith grows, the more our capacity to be
patient increases. This is important, because patience preserves
us from agitation, an emotion that can become devastating to
mind and body and to those who are near to us.

> Be patient, for thy Lord is Patient.[11]

> I can, on no account, feel impatient of the adversities that
> I have borne in my love for Thee.[12]

> He will, certainly, repay all them that endure with patience
> and put their confidence in Him.[13]

> Blessed are the steadfastly enduring, they that are patient
> under ills and hardships, who lament not over anything that
> befalleth them, and who tread the path of resignation.[14]

The virtues and attributes pertaining unto God are all evident and manifest, and have been mentioned and described in all the heavenly Books. Among them are trustworthiness, truthfulness, purity of heart while communing with God, forbearance, resignation to whatever the Almighty hath decreed, contentment with the things His Will hath provided, patience, nay, thankfulness in the midst of tribulation, and complete reliance, in all circumstances, upon Him. These rank, according to the estimate of God, among the highest and most laudable of all acts. All other acts are, and will ever remain, secondary and subordinate unto them . . .[15]

There can be no doubt that if we immerse ourselves in prayer we will be able to bear difficulties patiently. When we are patient we experience the omnipotent 'hand' of God helping us to solve our problems. But patience is not to be confused with passivity. If we sit in self-pity, waiting for something to happen, we don't allow our heart to receive the all-sufficing power which will influence our life.

Difficulties are hard to bear. If they were not, we would not be motivated to ask for divine assistance, and would neither experience those feelings of gratitude, love and realization that His response to our supplications generates within us, nor develop the virtue of faith, because faith arises from the recognition that relief of our pain will come – a recognition acquired thanks to all the previous tests in which we experienced relief.

Difficulties not only give us the opportunity to experience God's mercy in all its forms, but enable us to develop our virtues. Nevertheless, from the moment when our difficulties become hard to manage, it is then that the divine Word, which helps us and gives us solace when challenged by tests, is essential to the happiness of our soul.

When we are overcome by dismay, that is the moment to pass more time in prayer and meditation, and then act – for it is through action, placing ourselves at the service of others and concerning ourselves with their problems, that we forget our own, and even, perhaps, resolve them through such acts.

Heed not your weaknesses and frailty; fix your gaze upon the invincible power of the Lord, your God, the Almighty . . . Arise in His name, put your trust wholly in Him, and be assured of ultimate victory.[16]

10

THE VALUE OF STRUGGLE

To fight against ourselves is anything but easy. We tend (more or less unconsciously) to follow someone else, perhaps a 'teacher', in the hope of being 'saved'. But if that happens, the value of our struggle, which is essential, is lost.

'When we consider existence,' said 'Abdu'l-Bahá, 'we observe that the mineral, the vegetable, the animal, and the human realms, each and all, are in need of an educator . . . It is therefore clear and evident that man stands in need of an educator. This educator must undeniably be perfect in every way and distinguised above all men.'[1]

This emphasizes what Bahá'u'lláh writes in the Seven Valleys: ' the severed wayfarer – if invisible confirmation descend upon him and the Guardian of the Cause assist him – may cross these seven stages in seven steps, nay rather in seven breaths, nay rather in a single breath, if God will and desire it.' [2] This suggests that the seeker cannot enter the path of God without the support of an Educator who stands by him in his struggle to resolve problems, but not that the Educator is the one to resolve them.

Our essential self will be able to emerge only if we struggle, getting used to accepting conflicts and tests and considering them to be opportunities where we can learn, even if they may cause us pain. We should consider such struggle in its true perspective, welcoming it, because it enables us to 'meet' ourselves. Profound inner struggle is like 'juice' that only we ourselves can distil; it has great value and no-one can do this work for us.

Let us recall our reflections in the 'Intermezzo' on Jacob wrestling with the Angel of God. It is an unequal struggle, in that Jacob emerges from it crippled, but that is part of human nature. A person who does not face struggle courageously will not be able to 'meet' himself, since he will know neither his own limits nor his virtues that reflect the image of God within him.

Without such struggle, life has no flavour! Struggle is inner friction that makes our inner being ever sweeter. It's not a case of indulging our grief, or of deliberately seeking suffering, so much as assuming responsibility for facing whatever situations, whatever problems or conflicts that may present themselves on the path of life; it means being fully involved in life, whatever the situation, doing everything possible to truly live and know ourselves, because it is only in this way that we can become like firmly rooted trees. Therefore, when we have a problem let us not simply try to eliminate it, but let us try to learn through it, starting from where we are, and be able to understand that there will be a subsequent problem for us to overcome that represents a deeper aspect of ourselves. Friction burns away impurities, leaving only the authentic part of ourselves.

If we live the tests and difficult situations of life in this way, they will not be simply random, but will come to us as designed for us by our souls, for our guidance. To fight with ourselves doesn't mean making war on ourselves, but rather engaging in a process of understanding that demands faith, constancy and determination.[3] In the well-known words of the Polish poet Herbert Zbigniew: 'To get to the source we must swim against the current; only garbage goes with the flow.'

In recent years the Arabic word *jihad* has, sadly, become

well known for all the wrong reasons, becoming a synonym for violence and terrorism due to the circumstances in which it is generally used. Undeniably, various Surahs of the Qur'án talk about jihad as 'holy war' – but never with the sinister meaning attributed to it by Islamist fundamentalists. And nevertheless, it is also true that when the Qur'án speaks of the 'Great Jihad', the term always signifies a non-warlike 'effort', rather a 'struggle' with oneself. For example, in Surah 49 we read: 'The true believers are those only who believe in God and His Apostle, and afterwards doubt not; and who contend with their substance and their persons on the path of God. These are the sincere.'[4]

This is the true 'holy war' that every human being must fight, if he is not to be limited to living life as a 'happy vegetable' or a 'foolish saint', as Gurdjieff wrote.

There are only four instances in the Qur'án where the word 'jihad' is used. Nevertheless, in the huge bibliography on the subject, it is difficult to reconcile the generally accepted meaning of jihad/war with jihad/effort (more exactly 'targeted effort'), a task intended to give a positive meaning to the root *jihada*. But the expression 'targeted effort' indicates in the mystical sphere (and not only there), the 'great struggle' against one's own passions in the individual's path toward God.[5]

In this individual journey toward God it's important to 'know ourselves' and to 'live the life' we are given. With regard to this, I would like to share a personal experience that I expect many others have had too. I was in a shopping centre one day when my attention was drawn to a boy in a wheelchair, moving nimbly through the crowd. Although his hands were contorted and his limbs reduced to a skeleton covered with skin, he manoeuvred the wheelchair in which he was confined with strength and agility. When I at last summoned the courage to look into his eyes, I realized to my great astonishment that his face, serene and smiling, expressed a radiant joy that was in complete contrast to the tense faces of most of the other people around him, intent only on the race to grab the goods on offer.

From that boy I learnt a basic lesson, one that is well expressed by Rúḥíyyih Rabbani in her book *Prescription for Living*:

> If you are deficient or handicapped in some respect, surmount it; . . . cultivate your own gifts, whatever they may be . . and make your original disadvantage an asset by contrast. If you are ugly or homely, then offset it by being witty or intelligent or sweet-tempered, sympathetic and obliging. If you are deformed, forget it; let your other characteristics shine so brightly as to make your deformity merely a distinction – more, a cause for admiration.[6]

That boy, so affected by his unfortunate fate, had understood the value of the constant struggle required to 'live his own life', cultivating 'all his other gifts of mind and soul so thoroughly that his deformed body, far from being a disadvantage, seemed an endearing part of him'.[7]

Almost nothing is impossible of accomplishment. It is then impossible for the human race to be happy?

11

SERVICE

All are His servants . . .

We know that the station of service is the highest rank to which a believer can aspire.[1] True service implies action sustained by love. As 'Abdu'l-Bahá said: 'Spirituality is love in action.'[2] And Bahá'u'lláh writes:

> Let your principal concern be to rescue the fallen from the slough of impending extinction, and to help him embrace the ancient Faith of God. Your behaviour towards your neighbour should be such as to manifest clearly the signs of the one true God, for ye are the first among men to be re-created by His Spirit, the first to adore and bow the knee before Him, the first to circle round His throne of glory . . . Unloose your tongues, and proclaim unceasingly His Cause. This shall be better for you than all the treasures of the past and of the future, if ye be of them that comprehend this truth . . . Vie ye with each other in the service of God and of His Cause. This is indeed what profiteth you in this world, and in that which is to come.[3]

Let us consider again the tradition quoted by Bahá'u'lláh in *The Seven Valleys*: 'A servant is drawn unto Me in prayer until I answer him; and when I have answered him, I become the ear wherewith he heareth.'⁴

This is the moment of the soul's meeting with the Word of the Manifestation of God. As 'Abdu'l-Bahá writes :

> The blessings of Bahá'u'lláh are a shoreless sea, and even life everlasting is only a dewdrop therefrom. The waves of that sea are continually lapping against the hearts of the friends, and from those waves there come intimations of the spirit and ardent pulsings of the soul, until the heart giveth way, and willing or not, turneth humbly in prayer unto the Kingdom of the Lord.⁵

It is the moment of the second birth, writes Julio Savi.⁶ In that instant, the inner essence of man is regenerated. In one moment he glimpses the perfect individual and collective reality shown to him by the Manifestation of God, and through that vision a force is generated within him that can then guide him, for the rest of his life, over the thorny path of self-purification, of sacrifice, of love to the point of annihilation of his ego, to perfect service, to the stage of unconditional love.

In that meeting, then, the heart is transformed; feelings are recreated; the desire for action is born . . .

> An act, however infinitesimal, is, when viewed in the mirror of the knowledge of God, mightier than a mountain. Every drop proffered in His path is as the sea in that mirror.⁷

'The most meritorious of all deeds,'⁸ the greatest service, is to teach the Faith. Teaching the Faith brings the soul closer to God and thus also to our own selves, through recognition of the Manifestation of God and exposure to His life-giving influence.

O My Brother! A pure heart is as a mirror; cleanse it with the burnish of love and severance from all else save God, that the true sun may shine within it and the eternal morning dawn. Then wilt thou clearly see the meaning of 'Neither doth My earth nor My heaven contain Me, but the heart of My faithful servant containeth Me.' And thou will take up thy life in thine hand, and with infinite longing cast it before the new Beloved One.[9]

Those who recognize the Manifestation will consequently put themselves at the service of His primary purpose – the realization of the unity of the human race. Service is not abstract; it must be realized through acts of service to all mankind. Through this service believers learn to practise life's virtues and to continually perfect them. The behavioural model suggested by Bahá'u'lláh, the most succinct and perfect guide to character of a true human being, is summarized in this marvellous Tablet:

Be generous in prosperity, and thankful in adversity. Be worthy of the trust of thy neighbour, and look upon him with a bright and friendly face. Be a treasure to the poor, an admonisher to the rich, an answerer of the cry of the needy, a preserver of the sanctity of thy pledge. Be fair in thy judgement, and guarded in thy speech. Be unjust to no man, and show all meekness to all men. Be as a lamp unto them that walk in darkness, a joy to the sorrowful, a sea for the thirsty, a haven for the distressed, an upholder and defender of the victim of oppression. Let integrity and uprightness distinguish all thine acts. Be a home for the stranger, a balm to the suffering, a tower of strength for the fugitive. Be eyes to the blind, and a guiding light unto the feet of the erring. Be an ornament to the countenance of truth, a crown to the brow of fidelity, a pillar of the temple of righteousness, a breath of life to the body of mankind, an ensign of the hosts of justice, a luminary above the horizon of virtue, a dew to the soil of the human heart, an ark on the ocean of knowledge, a sun in the heaven of bounty, a gem on the diadem of wisdom, a shining light in the firmament of thy generation, a fruit upon the tree of humility.[10]

Or in this succinct and perfect guide for human beings in all their complexity:

Be united in counsel, be one in thought. Let each morn be better than its eve and each morrow richer than its yesterday. Man's merit lieth in service and virtue and not in the pageantry of wealth and riches. Take heed that your words be purged from idle fancies and worldly desires and your deeds be cleansed from craftiness and suspicion. Dissipate not the wealth of your precious lives in the pursuit of evil and corrupt affection, nor let your endeavours be spent in promoting your personal interest. Be generous in your days of plenty, and be patient in the hour of loss. Adversity is followed by success and rejoicings follow woe. Guard against idleness and sloth, and cling unto that which profiteth mankind, whether young or old, whether high or low. Beware lest ye sow tares of dissension among men or plant thorns of doubt in pure and radiant hearts.[11]

In this Day, teaching the Faith is considered so important as to be on the same level as the martyrdom of the early believers. Only the words of Bahá'u'lláh, the Báb and 'Abdu'l-Bahá can adequately express the value of this station:

O friends! Be not careless of the virtues with which ye have

86

been endowed, neither be neglectful of your high destiny . . . Ye are the stars of the heaven of understanding, the breeze that stirreth at the break of day, the soft-flowing waters upon which must depend the very life of all men . . .[12]

Ye are even as the fire which in the darkness of the night has been kindled upon the mountain-top. Let your light shine before the eyes of men . . . You are the salt of the earth, but if the salt have lost its savour, wherewith shall it be salted?[13]

Ye are the waves of the deep sea of knowledge . . . ye are the stars in the skies of God's compassion . . . ye are the clouds of divine pity over the gardens of life . . .

. . . In His bowers are ye the blossoms and sweet-smelling herbs, in the rose garden of the spirit the nightingales that utter plaintive cries. Ye are the birds that soar upward into the firmament of knowledge, the royal falcons on the wrist of God.

. . . Ye must shine forth like the lightning, and raise up a clamouring like unto the great sea. Like a candle must ye shed your light, and even as the soft breezes of God must ye blow across the world. Even as sweet breaths from heavenly bowers, as musk-laden winds from the gardens of the Lord, must ye perfume the air for the people of knowledge, and even as the splendours shed by the true Sun, must ye illumine the hearts of humankind. For ye are the life-laden winds, ye are the jessamine-scents from the gardens of the saved . . . In the darkness of the world be ye radiant flames; in the sands of perdition, be ye well-springs of the water of life . . . Now is the time to serve, now is the time to be on fire . . .

. . . We must gird ourselves for service, kindle love's

flame, and burn away in its heat. We must loose our tongues till we set the wide world's heart afire, and with bright rays of guidance blot out the armies of the night, and then, for His sake, on the field of sacrifice, fling down our lives.[14]

In the course of spiritual development, every Bahá'í encounters two essential conditions: the development of his or her character, and teaching activities. Teaching is an integral part of that obedience which will lead a believer to behave in a manner befitting the standards given to us by Bahá'u'lláh. And obedience on the part of the believer goes far beyond merely 'right conduct' to include an active role in the teaching work.

Of all the gifts of God the greatest is the gift of Teaching. It draweth unto us the Grace of God and is our first obligation. Of such a gift how we deprive ourselves?[15]

God hath prescribed unto every one the duty of teaching His Cause. Whoever ariseth to discharge this duty, must needs, ere he proclaimeth His Message, adorn himself with the ornament of an upright and praiseworthy character, so that his words may attract the hearts of such as are receptive to his call. Without it, he can never hope to influence his hearers.[16]

The length of the road we must walk on our approach to the Kingdom of God depends on us. It may be made shorter through submission to the will of God and teaching the Faith. Each one of us is a unique teacher, since no two people teach in exactly the same way. Because of this, every one of us has the capability to reach certain people who could not be reached by others in order to share the message with them. And this is thanks to our work, our studies, our unique talents and even our weaknesses and our problems, which have all forged this capability. Each one of us thus bears a huge responsibility!

Transmitting the message of Bahá'u'lláh doesn't require a group of experts; each person has his own role and his own responsibility. All that is asked is to teach according to one's own capacity, putting all one's trust in Bahá'u'lláh in the certainty of receiving His assistance. If we persevere in the teaching work, the combination of our own efforts and the assistance we receive will continually increase our capacities.

The Pen of the Most High hath decreed and imposed upon every one the obligation to teach this Cause . . . God will, no doubt, inspire whosoever detacheth himself from all else but Him, and will cause the pure waters of wisdom and utterance to gush out and flow copiously from his heart . . .

Wert thou to consider this world, and realize how fleeting are the things that pertain unto it, though wouldst choose to tread no path except the path of service to the Cause of thy Lord. None would have the power to deter thee from celebrating his praise, though all men should arise to oppose thee.[17]

Arise thou to serve the Cause of thy Lord; then give the people the joyful tidings concerning this resplendent Light whose revelation hath been announced by God through His Prophets and Messengers. Admonish everyone moreover to observe prudence as ordained by Him, and in the Name of God advise them, saying: It behoveth every one in this Day of God to dedicate himself to the teaching of the Cause with utmost prudence and steadfastness. Should he discover a pure soil, let him sow the seed of the Word of God, otherwise it would be preferable to observe silence.[18]

Whoso openeth his lips in this Day and maketh mention of the name of his Lord, the hosts of Divine inspiration shall descend upon him from the heaven of My name, the All-Knowing, the All-Wise.[19]

Centre your attention unceasingly upon that which will cause the Word of God to be exalted. In this Most Great Revelation goodly deeds and a praiseworthy character are regarded as the hosts of God, likewise is His blessed and holy Word. These hosts are the lodestone of the hearts of men and the effective means for unlocking doors. Of all the weapons in the world this is the keenest.[20]

12

OBEDIENCE AND SUBMISSION

. . . and all abide by His bidding!

Submitting oneself to the Will of God requires time and sacrifice. In general, we arrive at obedience in one of two ways: either we are forced into it by hard tests, or we have become conscious that this is the way to our true happiness – in other words, the happiness that nothing and no-one can undermine. The struggle is with ourselves, because it's up to us, on a daily basis and according to the level of our obedience, to decide what part of ourselves we are ready to sacrifice in order to surrender to the Will of God and place ourselves in the service of the purpose He has ordained for us.

This is the true significance of the 'Great Jihad' as understood in Qur'án 49:15. This is the struggle Shoghi Effendi is referring to, when he writes that every Bahá'í must struggle and win the victory over himself. And that it is only when he has conquered himself that he becomes a true instrument in the service of the Cause of God, and not before. And that he will not enjoy great success until he has done this.

A person who perceives that spiritual joy derives from such an act of submission will be less reluctant to submit himself, and in progressing, will also learn that submission consists not only in carrying out the Will of God, but in carrying it out with enthusiasm and gratitude. Only in this way can happiness be found. God wants man to be happy, and it is for this purpose that He has given man a soul that rejoices in giving up its own will to that of the Creator. To experience this happiness, above all in difficult moments, helps to drive us forward, taking another step towards ever greater obedience, leaving an even greater part of ourselves behind in order to create space for the love of God.

The perfect example comes to us from 'Abdu'l-Bahá, the Servant of the Glory, when He describes the two years spent in the Prison of 'Akká:

> I was very happy all the time, because I was a free man. Shut off in that room, my spirit travelled throughout the immensity of space.
>
> The soul of man must be happy no matter where he is. One must attain to that condition of inward beatitude and peace – then outward circumstances will not alter his spiritual calmness and joyousness.[1]

Personal problems and unpleasant situations over which we have no direct control can discourage us and lead to self-pity. It is always a good idea to analyse the situation. If some possibility to remove pain exists, then it is useless to worry, because this is an answer. If there is no solution, there is still no need to worry, because we cannot do otherwise than to place ourselves in God's hands, since He alone can remove difficulties.

Through submission we may discover that our problems can be resolved, or at least rendered no longer intolerable. When we put less emphasis on the actual events and on our sadness, we leave room for reconciliation whenever we will be able to show our gratitude for those gifts that have been given to us. Feelings of anger, fear, pain, despair and self-pity are changed into appreciation, strength, creativity, joy, kindness and the desire to serve. These qualities are necessary if we want to reduce negative emotions. When things are going well, we often forget these virtues, so it is when we run into problems, when we are suffering, that we can best learn them. The traits of the material world are transformed into spiritual qualities and, through persevering in this choice, we reach further stages of inner peace, serenity, compassion and spiritual happiness.

> O My servants! Sorrow not if, in these days and on this earthly plane, things contrary to your wishes have been ordained and manifested by God, for days of blissful joy, of heavenly delight, are assuredly in store for you. Worlds, holy and spiritually glorious, will be unveiled to your eyes. You are destined by Him, in this world and hereafter, to partake of their benefits, to share in their joys, and to obtain a portion of their sustaining grace. To each and every one of them you will, no doubt, attain.[2]

There is a close relationship between obedience and submission, in that obedience both precedes and follows submission. The seeker passes through several stages of obedience before arriving at submission. One can be relatively obedient without being submissive, while submission includes obedience. Obedience has the connotation of fulfilling a task; submission of answering a desire. An obedient person does 'what he is asked to do'; a person who voluntarily submits himself does 'what he wants to do, what he longs to do'. Before submission, obedience competes with the ego and with materialistic values in the choices we make, but after submitting, obedience becomes a preference, carried out not just because we have so decided but above all so that we may not be deprived of the love of God which fills us with joy. We voluntarily try not to make decisions that might deprive us of this good, until obedience becomes a spontaneous act – even if in reality it can never be completely spontaneous, since absolute spontaneity in obedience can only result from total submission, and only the Manifestation of God is capable of that.

It is through obedience that the seeker develops the faculties of his soul, but with this difference: before submitting himself this development is slow and subject to continual stops and starts, while after submission the rate of growth not only increases, but the seeker 'sees with the eyes and hears with the ears' of his Lord, desiring nothing other than to serve Him. As Proust is often quoted as writing: 'The real voyage of discovery consists not in seeking new landscapes, but in having new eyes.'³ According to Bahá'í teaching,

> Depth of belief is assured by the inner transformation, that salutary acquisition of spiritual and moral character, which is the outcome of obedience to the divine laws and principles. ⁴

> So great shall be the discernment of this seeker that he will discriminate between truth and falsehood, even as he doth distinguish the sun from shadow. If in the uttermost corners of the East the sweet savours of God be wafted, he will assuredly recognize and inhale their fragrance, even though he be dwelling in the uttermost ends of the West. He will, likewise, clearly distinguish all the signs of God – His wondrous utterances, His great works, and mighty deeds – from the doings, the words and ways of men, even as the jeweller who knoweth the gem from the stone, or the man who distinguisheth the spring from autumn, and heat from cold. When the channel of the human soul is cleansed of all worldly and impeding attachments, it will unfailingly perceive the breath of the Beloved across immeasurable

distances, and will, led by its perfume, attain and enter the City of Certitude.[5]

Further, it is only by sanctifying our souls 'of all worldly and impeding attachments' that we will be able to remember 'that true and radiant morn' when, gathered in His presence we listened awestruck, as He 'gave utterance to these three most holy words':

O friends! Prefer not your will to Mine; never desire that which I have not desired for you, and approach Me not with lifeless hearts, defiled with worldly desires and cravings.

And Bahá'u'lláh promises us: 'Would ye but sanctify your souls, ye would at this present hour recall that place and those surroundings, and the truth of My utterance should be made evident unto all of you.'[6]

13

JOY AND PAIN

Bahá'u'lláh tells us that 'the human soul is, in its essence . . .
a mystery among His mysteries'[1] and that, as a spiritual entity
created by God and emanating from Him, man is inhabited by
the divine spirit, and this is his true reality.[2]

Although emanating from God, every human soul is
an individual, in other words, every soul is characterized by
certain potential qualities that are unique to that individual
and which in the course of his existence on this earth he will
be asked to bring to realization.

In the process of developing individuality in this world,
a soul is influenced by two equally active realities: its divine
nature which urges it to develop its potential spiritual qualities, and the material nature of human beings which drives
them to indulge their natural emotions. The development of
spiritual potentialities can therefore take place only through a
conscious effort of will that makes every individual responsible
for what he is, in the circumstances in which he finds himself.

The soul operates in the physical world through the body,
and at the same time makes use of it for its own development.
Just as the body possesses certain faculties, so too the soul is
endowed with infinite gifts or faculties.

We may think of this – to take an example – as being given,
in the first moments of our existence, a construction kit for a
revolving mirror, together with all the instructions necessary to

make it work. The instructions for use are regularly updated, and the kit also carries an absolute guarantee that it will work perfectly so long as we scrupulously follow the instructions.

This mirror is our soul, whose source of energy is a battery we call 'spirit', and whose functioning is controlled by the mind, which contains all the data. The instructions represent the sacred texts, continually updated by the Messengers of God.

To the individual is left the liberty, and thus also the responsibility, of orienting the mirror either upwards to reflect heavenly qualities, or downwards to reflect material values. Turning the mirror upwards implies turning ourselves towards our spiritual nature; turning it downwards implies choosing material traits. Both choices demand a sacrifice that can lead to suffering as well as happiness, but while the first is a spiritual happiness, the second is material.

So what's the difference? Material happiness is associated with self-gratification and gratification of the senses, while spiritual happiness is the love of God felt in the depths of one's soul. Material happiness is recognizable through feelings, while spiritual happiness is perceived only through the *inner eye* which is a faculty of the soul. Material happiness is transitory and fleeting, while spiritual happiness is a prevailing force that will not be hidden, and that literally removes feelings of sadness, despair and fear. So it's not a case of being less sad or less fearful, but of replacing sadness and fear with joy and courage; replacing hatred with love. In the words of 'Abdu'l-Bahá: 'A thought of hatred must be destroyed by a more powerful thought of love.'[3] And Bahá'u'lláh writes:

> . . . inasmuch as He, in token of His mercy unto thee, hath turned thy sorrow into gladness, and transmuted thy grief into blissful joy.[4]

Man achieves this kind of happiness only through obedience to the Word of God and the consequent development bringing his spirit – thanks to the Spirit of Faith – into relationship with the Holy Spirit manifested by Bahá'u'lláh: 'From sorrow he turneth to bliss, from anguish to joy.'[5]

A person who senses that spiritual happiness results from acts of submission will overcome his reluctance to submit himself, as we have seen in the previous chapter. Such a person will have learnt that submission implies not only carrying out the Will of God, but carrying it out with thankfulness, raising praises to God (*Praised be God! . . . All are His servants, and all abide by His bidding!*).

Praise alone is not sufficient, and nor is gratitude alone. It is only when they are carried out together that they bring with them instant joy and happiness.

'Abdu'l-Bahá said: 'In this world we are influenced by two sentiments, Joy and Pain.'[6] And this theme of joy and pain is further expressed by that fine poet Kahlil Gibran:

Your joy is your sorrow unmasked.

And the selfsame well from which your laughter rises was oftentimes filled with your tears.

How else can it be?

The deeper the sorrow carves into your being, the more joy you can contain.

Is not the cup that holds your wine the very cup that was burned in the potter's oven?

And is not the lute that soothes your spirit the very wood that was hollowed with knives?

When you are joyous, look deep into your heart and you shall find it is only that which has given you sorrow that is giving you joy.

When you are sorrowful, look again into your heart,

and you shall see that in truth you are weeping for that which has been your delight.

Some of you say, 'Joy is greater than sorrow,' and others say, 'Nay, sorrow is the greater.'

But I say unto you, they are inseparable.

Together they come, and when one sits alone with you at your board, remember that the other is asleep upon your bed.

Verily you are suspended like scales between your sorrow and your joy.[7]

Spiritual happiness is not transitory; it knows no limits, in contrast with material happiness which soon leaves us dissatisfied. There is a process of growth that carries us from a lower to a higher level in infinite progression. In the words of 'Abdu'l-Bahá,

> Joy gives us wings! In times of joy our strength is more vital, our intellect keener, and our understanding less clouded.[8]

To be spiritually happy implies having certitude, serenity and radiance; it implies detachment from the material world and attachment to the Kingdom. It implies serving one's neighbour and trying to give some moments of happiness to others. We will then feel that our life is purposeful, a feeling that is deeply satisfying to the mind; in helping others we become happy ourselves.

> Peace of mind is gained by the centering of the spiritual consciousness on the Prophet of God; therefore you should study the spiritual Teachings, and receive the Water of Life from the Holy Utterances. Then by translating these high ideals into action, your entire character will be changed,

and your mind will not only find peace, but your entire being will find joy and enthusiasm.[9]

As to spiritual happiness, this is the true basis of the life of man, for life is created for happiness, not for sorrow; for pleasure, not for grief. Happiness is life; sorrow is death. Spiritual happiness is life eternal. This is a light which is not followed by darkness. This is an honour which is not followed by shame. This is a life that is not followed by death. This is an existence that is not followed by annihilation. This great blessing and precious gift is obtained by man only through the guidance of God . . .

This happiness is the fundamental basis from which man is created, worlds are originated, the contingent beings have existence and the world of God appears like unto the appearance of the sun at midday.

This happiness is but the love of God . . .

Were it not for this happiness the world of existence would not have been created.[10]

The blessings showered on those who have submitted themselves to the Will of God are much greater than simply reward for their services. The rewards we receive are always greater than our service, so that our thanks are never in proportion to the blessings received. So, in praying 'Is there any Remover of difficulties save God?' we ask God to help us to remove the veils that are entangled in our heart and preventing us from being truly thankful and happy for all the gifts He showers on each one of us in his munificence.

14

THE PATH THAT LEADS TO HAPPINESS

'One of the paradoxes of human life is that development of the self comes primarily through commitment to larger undertakings in which the self – even if only temporarily – is forgotten . . . To exalt such goals as acquisition and self-assertion as the purpose of life is to promote chiefly the animal side of human nature.'[1] In contrast, our goal is to develop all the attributes – the virtues – of our spiritual nature. Bahá'u'lláh writes: 'O friends! Be not careless of the virtues with which ye have been endowed, neither be neglectful of your high destiny.'[2]

The acquisition of one virtue necessarily leads to the development of all the others, since they are all linked, indissolubly interwoven. Everything in this world develops in clear relation to its component parts. This equilibrium is absolutely essential in life, whether on the biological or the spiritual level. Moderation in all things is necessary: just as we shouldn't give ourselves indigestion in relation to food, equally we shouldn't do so with prayer.

What we need, then, is to learn more about the spiritual laws of how to live life – those things that are good for our development and what we must do to enjoy not just a 'healthy mind in a healthy body' but also a healthy soul in a strong spirit. And for the soul to be spiritually healthy it must be in harmony, consciously and dynamically, with its Creator.

Ruḥíyyih Rabbani, in her book *Prescription for Living*, writes that 'the road to happiness' is paved with virtues that may be considered to be the solid foundations of 'good character'. 'Abdu'l-Bahá defines them as *the seven qualifications of the divinely enlightened soul*:

1. Knowledge. Man must attain the knowledge of God.

2. Faith.

3. Steadfastness.

4. Truthfulness. Truthfulness is the foundation of all the virtues of the world of humanity. Without truthfulness, progress and success in all of the worlds of God are impossible for a soul. When this holy attribute is established in man, all the divine qualities will also become realized.

5. Uprightness. And this is one of the greatest divine attainments.

6. Fidelity. This is also a beautiful trait of the heavenly man.

7. Evanescence or Humility. That is to say, man must become evanescent in God. Must forget his own selfish conditions that he may thus arise to the station of sacrifice . . .[3]

But, Rabbani writes,

> they might be called the 'cold virtues'; absolutely essential though they are, they are also absolutely insufficient for the formation of a noble human being. The 'warm virtues'

must be added to them . . . Our representative man so far is truthful, honest, upright and reliable. He is like a marble statue, perfect but inanimate. Warmth must flush his heart and veins, colour come up in his skin, his arteries must throb, his limbs move. Kindness is what is needed.[4]

The Bahá'í Writings have much to say on this virtue:

O Son of Spirit! My first counsel is this: Possess a pure, kindly and radiant heart, that thine may be a sovereignty ancient, imperishable and everlasting.[5]

Be ye sincerely kind, not in appearance only. [6]

O ye lovers of God! Be kind to all peoples; care for every person; do all ye can to purify the hearts and minds of men; strive ye to gladden every soul. To every meadow be a shower of grace, to every tree the water of life; be as sweet musk to the sense of humankind, and to the ailing be a fresh, restoring breeze. Be pleasing waters to all those who thirst, a careful guide to all who have lost their way; be father and mother to the orphan, be loving sons and daughters to the old, be an abundant treasure to the poor. Think ye of love and good fellowship as the delights of heaven, think ye of hostility and hatred as the torments of hell.[7]

Kindness is the rain that refreshes, that gives life, that cleans and blesses. And, as Rabbani writes: 'To kindness should be added those tender passions that are among the distinguishing features of the human race: sympathy, compassion, under-standing, forgiveness, generosity . . .'[8]

Another of the 'warm' virtues is courtesy. Bahá'u'lláh writes:

O people of God! I admonish you to observe courtesy. For above all else it is the prince of virtues. Well is it with him who is illumined with the light of courtesy and is attired with the vesture of uprightness. Whoso is endued with courtesy hath indeed attained a sublime station.[9]

Commenting on the virtue of courtesy, Rabbani writes:

> . . . manners are the little kindnesses of life. Everything is better in this world for receiving certain finishing touches: gems are first cut and then polished; furniture is planed and then stained and varnished; clothes are cut and sewn, but they are also neatly hemmed and embellished . . . Courtesy is the equivalent in our characters of these finishing touches.[10]

Courtesy makes our relationships with others smoother. 'Do you like people who look sour? Hostile? Angry?', asks Rabbani.[11] Even if such may be only one's outward appearance, it nevertheless expresses something of the inner being – a lack of well-being, jealousy, repressed hatred – and this can influence other people. It's therefore important to remedy the situation. If a sad expression stems from illness, we should look after ourselves and seek healing, but in the meantime we can also make a small effort to remove the antisocial expression from our face and substitute it with a smile instead; not only will this do us no harm but it might even help us feel better. In seeking to appear a bit more cheerful and serene, we actually feel more cheerful and serene.

> Verily the most necessary thing is contentment under all circumstances; by this one is preserved from morbid conditions and from lassitude. Yield not to grief and sorrow:

they cause the greatest misery. Jealousy consumeth the body and anger doth burn the liver: avoid these two as you would a lion.[12]

'We live in a rather rushed, tired, worried world these days,' writes Rabbani. 'When our eyes fall on a tranquil or smiling face it produces a feeling of assuagement, however infinitesimal.'[13] If, for instance, participants in a devotional meeting are wearing long faces, guests may feel uncomfortable, while in the presence of radiant faces they will experience joy and tranquillity. Although this is just a small and easily removed difficulty, let's remember that life gives us back what we put in.

To conclude this brief look at the 'warm virtues', we must inevitably mention the virtue of mildness.

'Blessed are the meek,' says the Gospel of Matthew, 'for they shall inherit the earth.' Meek people sometimes appear to be melancholy or depressed, but in fact they fall into depression in order to free themselves from the overwhelming emotion of sadness. When we observe those who are meek but melancholy we can see that they are similar to those who are meek but happy, in that they follow the same path, freeing themselves from wild emotion. Meekness, therefore, instils a sense of security and serenity, and consequently warmth.

Those who are meek know how to empty themselves, how to renounce their own desires while simultaneously loving unconditionally and infinitely, as Jesus did. The meek are the 'poor in spirit' who, being such, know how to stretch out their hands to others, who know how to pray and how to be the 'least ones' on the earth, in the sense that they know how to free their minds from all human knowledge so that they can be entirely filled by grace. Leaving behind human knowledge, in exchange they receive heavenly understanding.

If I have dwelt on discussing joy and happiness, it is because

I am convinced that the purpose of all prayer is to guide us on our path and give us the spiritual energy necessary to achieve true happiness.

Simply 'removing difficulties' is not necessarily synonymous with happiness. It can give us a certain amount of relief, even joy, but this is only temporary. Happiness – true happiness – is won every day through a journey that is often long and strewn with obstacles. 'Man is, in reality, a spiritual being,' said 'Abdu'l-Bahá, 'and only when he lives in the spirit is he truly happy.'[14]

And so the Báb's prayer is not limited to the first plea for help, for He wishes us to be truly happy and not merely relieved of our tests and difficulties, however right it is to ask for divine assistance. Instead, He invites us to bear witness in an act of faith (*He is God!*), to praise God (*Praised be God!*) and to accept to submit ourselves to His Will (*all abide by His bidding*). And this because only by observing His commandments is it possible to achieve happiness:

> Whoso keepeth the commandments of God shall attain everlasting felicity.[15]

And what is the best way to serve (*all are His servants*) in putting these commandments into practice? The Bahá'í Writings tell us:

> The service of the friends belongs to God, not to them. Strive to become a source of harmony, spirituality and joyfulness to the hearts of the friends . . .[16]

> That one indeed is a man who, today, dedicateth himself to the service of the entire human race.[17]

. . . all effort and exertion put forth by man from the fullness of his heart is worship, if it is prompted by the highest motives and the will to do service to humanity. This is worship: to serve mankind and to minister to the need of the people. Service is prayer.[18]

God be thanked, we have 'Abdu'l-Bahá, to whom we can relate in every situation – He Who, in his meeting with Bahá'ís, indicated many times the high road that every individual should follow if he really wishes to carry out the Will of God, to fully realize the purpose of his own existence and consequently his true happiness:

You must manifest complete love and affection toward all mankind. Do not exalt yourselves above others, but consider all as your equals, recognizing them as the servants of one God. Know that God is compassionate toward all; therefore, love all from the depths of your hearts, prefer all religionists before yourselves, be filled with love for every race, and be kind toward the people of all nationalities. Never speak disparagingly of others, but praise without distinction. Pollute not your tongues by speaking evil of another. Recognize your enemies as friends, and consider those who wish you evil as the wishers of good. You must not see evil as evil and then compromise with your opinion, for to treat in a smooth, kindly way one whom you consider evil or an enemy is hypocrisy, and this is not worthy or allowable. You must consider your enemies as your friends, look upon your evil-wishers as your well-wishers and treat them accordingly. Act in such a way that your heart may be free from hatred. Let not your heart be offended with anyone. If someone commits an error and wrong toward you, you must instantly forgive him. Do not complain of others. Refrain from reprimanding them, and if you wish to give admonition or advice, let it be offered in such a way that it will not burden the bearer. Turn all your thoughts toward bringing joy to hearts. Beware! Beware! Lest ye offend any heart. Assist the world of humanity as much as possible. Be the source of consolation to every sad one, assist every weak one, be helpful to every indigent one, care for every sick one, be the cause of glorification to every lowly one, and shelter those who are overshadowed by fear.

In brief, let each one of you be as a lamp shining forth with the light of the virtues of the world of humanity. Be trustworthy, sincere, affectionate and replete with chastity. Be illumined, be spiritual, be divine, be glorious, be quickened of God, be a Bahá'í.[19]

15

IS THERE ROOM FOR DOUBT?

The more our faith ripens, the less it is touched by anxiety, effort, doubt. But since there is no ripening of faith without questions, a claim to believe (or not to believe) without difficulty, never having known the challenge of doubt, may be viewed with scepticism. When confronted with life events and above all with suffering, any debate on the subject, no matter how clear, risks staying at the level of discussion without ever emerging from the shadows of doubt.[1]

The development of religious faith implies leaving old habits behind and being willing to risk anxiety and uncertainty, inevitable passages in the crisis of growth. And as we have seen, 'crisis' can be understood as 'choice, trial, opportunity'.

A certain amount of doubt is a path leading to truth; above all, it saves us from that dangerous absolute fixation on our own views that leads to arrogance and an even more dangerous fanaticism. It usually begins with 'I believe' but with a suspicion that we have no mastery in our belief. This phase is not yet the stage of true faith, for true faith derives not from a will to believe, but from knowledge. It is when we know *why* we believe that we can claim to have faith. Yet even knowledge can sometimes be touched by doubt as long as it has not become a continuous knowing – for 'a little knowledge is a dangerous thing'. We need to 'know that we know': that is, to have true learning, which is not mere knowledge, but knowledge steeped in wisdom. It is then that our faith becomes certitude, a certitude that only the heart can perceive after the profound 'suffering' of doubt which has fed the virtue of humility, the antithesis of arrogance.

Bahá'u'lláh thus admonishes us:

> Do thou beseech God to enable thee to remain steadfast in this path, and to aid thee to guide the peoples of the world to Him Who is the manifest and sovereign Ruler, Who hath revealed Himself in a distinct attire, Who giveth utterance to a Divine and specific Message. This is the essence of faith and certitude.[2]

With a few exceptions, doubt is not negative in itself, so long as we are aware of our own limitations, if we get rid of our bravado and arrogance and accept our own shortcomings and those of others. From this point of view, doubt is not a weakness, but a strength that stimulates awareness and knowledge.

Difficulties often arise when our personal conceptions do not coincide with what the Manifestations of God are asking of us, and we then find ourselves facing a choice between our own subjective ideas and divine revelation. This gives us the opportunity to overcome our own ego.

To call oneself a believer implies absolutes that are not easy. Sometimes we are in the presence of God, at other times we risk losing Him, or even 'fight' with Him. It's not easy to believe in a God of love when we think of the enormous amount of suffering in the world. It's easier to imagine a God Who is indifferent or even cruel, and it's unsurprising that a serious disaster or intense sorrow can overshadow faith. It isn't the actual gravity of a situation that counts, so much as the way in which it affects the individual who is going through it.

For example, a parent whose child dies will be overcome by

a sense of powerlessness. (At such a time, unfortunately, there will be other people who feel they can 'share' in such grief and insist on blathering on about it when they have no right to do so.) But in this experience of such profound grief there isn't even a word to describe parents whose child has died; a child who has lost its parents is defined as an orphan; someone who has lost a spouse is described as a widow or widower. The loss of one's child remains an insuperable sorrow that cannot be described. But it is necessary to try and see it as though finding oneself in the midst of a fire, surrounded by flames. The only thing to do is to jump through it, in the thought that: 'Perhaps there's a meadow over there, maybe if I make a huge leap I can (re-)sow the seed of my life there.'

Those who have been through such a disaster may well say, 'It's easy to talk when you haven't experienced it!' This is true! As has been said, the pain of others is always only half a pain. In all humility, we need to enfold in a tender embrace and with all our affection those who have been struck down by such misfortune.

A huge effort of will is needed to accept such things even when we can't understand them. 'The unknowable is within us and surrounds us,' according to ancient wisdom. If God were fully comprehensible to the mind, He would not be God, or man would in his turn be divine.

In discussing the various kinds of affliction (see Chapter 6) we have seen that the logic of divine love is not always accessible to human knowledge. But God takes care of His creatures when pain strikes without warning in bitter tests which at the time seem negative, but which often provide the stimulus for a change for the better or turn out to be healing medicine: 'outwardly it is fire and vengeance, but inwardly it is light and mercy'.[3] We can only see this point of view after we have processed our pain, after an existential struggle has been carried out, because everything that we leave behind will sooner or later catch up with us and, if it hasn't been dealt with, will continue to cause suffering.

This is the path of the 'Seven Valleys' we must traverse, step by step, if we want our search to lead us to 'true poverty and absolute nothingness'.[4] The traveller 'unaware of himself' in the Valley of Love, who 'seeth neither ignorance nor knowledge, neither doubt nor certitude' must enter the Valley of Knowledge and 'come out of doubt into certitude'.[5] But in the Valley of True Poverty and Absolute Nothingness, Bahá'u'lláh counsels us:

> If any of the utterances of this Servant may not be comprehended, or may lead to perturbation, the same must be inquired of again, that no doubt may linger, and the meaning be clear as the Face of the Beloved One shining from the 'Glorious Station'.
>
> These journeys have no visible ending in the world of time, but the severed wayfarer – if invisible confirmation descend upon him … [once again: 'Is there any Remover …'] – may cross these seven stages in seven steps, nay rather in seven breaths, nay rather in a single breath, if God will and desire it.[6]

The objective is inner serenity, rather than happiness. It can be assumed that everyone seeks to live their own life to the full, but in this world every human being ends up making mistakes that are the main cause of his or her problems. Every experience is valuable; we need to harvest them since they help us to examine ourselves and identify our own weaknesses. Nothing is lost in this life – not the least fragment of love, of sacrifice and of tears. Everything contributes to making us the unique person that God has created.

Those who are most serene are those who have become aware of the negative parts of themselves and, accepting them, have become able to control them, to master them, to make them better. The more we know our own limits, the more we become tolerant of those of others.

Spiritual life is fraught with difficulties created by human beings themselves. But spirituality goes beyond this; it implies the capacity to let the events of the world go by, living them without holding on to them. Spirituality stems from our inner being; it lives within us as a fruit of long and tiring self-conquest, to be made in silence and humility.

16

A SHORT SUMMING UP . . .

The importance of the message contained in a prayer is certainly not to be judged by the length of the prayer. All revealed prayers – precisely because they are revealed – are beyond the ability of man to judge. In reality, every single verse, even every single syllable, is invested with full significance and power. Short prayers such as the Báb's 'Is there any Remover of difficulties . . .' or the short Obligatory Prayer 'I bear witness, O my God . . .' revealed by Bahá'u'lláh, contain in their few lines the choice Wine, a compendium of fundamental verities whose essence every man must make an effort to grasp.

'Is there any Remover of difficulties save God?' expresses in rhetorical form complete faith in the omnipotence of God as the one Resolver of every difficulty that He may be pleased to resolve. At the same time, it expresses the love of God for his creatures, a love that will without a shadow of doubt guide them and help them to remove difficulties, even when it may seem to man, because of his own limitations, that God is not interested in him. There are times when we are unaware that divine help is at our side always, even if not in the form we desire, but this is because only God knows, in His inscrutable wisdom and omniscience, what is good for us. We often ask for things that in fact could result in major harm.

To understand that God is helping us in the best of all possible ways, and in order to act in consequence so that we may receive his gifts, we need to turn our hearts to Him in praise (*Praised be God!*), in complete faith that there is no other God but Him (*He is God!*).

'Be generous in prosperity, and thankful in adversity' – these poetic words open the Tablet of Bahá'u'lláh.[1] But all too often, instead of being generous for the gifts they have received, those who are prosperous become ever more greedy, forgetting both God and their neighbour: love for God is expressed in love for others. It ought to be natural that those who have received many gifts share them with those less fortunate, and there are indeed some who – often anonymously – make the effort to lighten the load of others. But unfortunately these people are rare enough to be called 'angels' rather than true human beings.

If it's true that 'he who finds a friend finds a treasure', it's also true that 'he who finds a treasure is remembered by his friends' – but often the rich find it easy to forget the poor! Twenty per cent of the world population live in relative prosperity, mostly forgetting to be generous, while their wealth is often amassed to the detriment of the remaining 80 per cent. It's usually only when we are struck by adversity that we remember God and our neighbour, either to ask for help (which although not a sign of spiritual maturity, at least means that we become 'acceptable' in terms of the general human position of weakness), or reacting by blaming others and particularly God for our misfortune, sometimes violently. In contrast, it's often those to whom life has reserved all kinds of difficulties and suffering who know how to be truly generous and thankful. So it's not by chance that Bahá'u'lláh's Tablet begins with the invitation to be 'generous in prosperity, and thankful in adversity'.

All we are asked to do is to open our hearts, that they may be filled with the grace of God. God loves us because it is in His nature to love us, just as the sun shines because its nature is to shine. In order to receive the rays of the sun, a plant turns its leaves toward it, and in the same way we must turn our hearts to the Manifestation of God in order to receive divine love. This is the purpose of our life, remembered each day in the short Obligatory Prayer:

> I bear witness, O my God, that Thou hast created me to know Thee and to worship Thee. I testify, at this moment, to my powerlessness and to Thy might, to my poverty and to Thy wealth.
> There is none other God but Thee, the Help in Peril, the Self-Subsisting.

From the moment that we testify 'to my powerlessness and to Thy might, to my poverty and to Thy wealth' it becomes right and natural to turn ourselves to God, He Who is the Omnipotent, Who knows all we truly need, Who will help to remove our true difficulties – those that form a veil between us and His Manifestation – so that we may 'know and worship' Him, something that goes well beyond simple acceptance. The road is that of obedience, in that 'all are His servants, and all abide by His bidding'. In fact, Bahá'u'lláh asks of us two basic things:

> The beginning of all things is the knowledge of God, and the end of all things is strict observance of whatsoever hath been sent down from the empyrean of the Divine Will that pervadeth all that is in the heavens and all that is on the earth.[2]

We know that we can have no knowledge of God except through knowing His Manifestation and observing the laws He has revealed. So the highest station man can reach is that of service: 'all are His servants,' since it is only through service that we can put into practice our faith, our love for God in the person of His Manifestation, our love for others and for ourselves. In choosing this path we will develop those talents or virtues that will be useful to us both in this world and the next.

To take an example: we may know everything about honey – its history, how bees produce it, the various kinds of honey and all their properties. We may have read everything there is to read about this amazing food, but until we put a drop – even a tiny bit – on our tongue and taste it, we will never be able to know what it really is.

> How great the multitude of truths which the garment of words can never contain! How vast the number of such verities as no expression can adequately describe, whose significance can never be unfolded, and to which not even the remotest allusions can be made! How manifold are the truths which must remain unuttered until the appointed time is come! Even as it has been said: 'Not everything that a man knoweth can be disclosed, nor can everything that he can disclose be regarded as timely, nor can every timely utterance be considered as suited to the capacity of those who hear it.'[3]

Nevertheless, beyond all analysis, all comparison, all other considerations, the best of all things remains – to reflect and meditate in the privacy of our own room, and with a free mind and a pure heart let every single word of the prayer descend as lifeblood into the depths of our being. Only in this way can we discover places and feelings that neither our eyes nor any of our other senses can perceive, for as we have so often reminded ourselves in this little book, it is through prayer that we begin to see with the eye of God and hear through His ears: 'A servant is drawn unto Me in prayer until I answer him and when I have answered him, I become the ear wherewith he heareth.'[4]

Cause me to taste, O my Lord, the divine sweetness of Thy remembrance and praise. . . . Inspire then my soul, O my God, with Thy wondrous remembrance, that I may glorify Thy name. Number me not with them who read Thy words and fail to find Thy hidden gift which, as decreed by Thee, is contained therein, and which quickeneth the souls of Thy creatures and the hearts of Thy servants. Cause me, O my Lord, to be reckoned among them who have been so stirred up by the sweet savours that have been wafted in Thy days that they have laid down their lives for Thee and hastened to the scene of their death in their longing to gaze on Thy beauty and in their yearning to attain Thy presence. And were any one to say unto them on their way, 'Whither go ye?' they would say, 'Unto God, the All-Possessing, the Help in Peril, the Self-Subsisting!'⁵

And finally: we have also touched on the subject of doubt, and the value of knowledge in overcoming it, but with reference to a knowledge illuminated by wisdom that leads to mysticism. It is on this path that doubt is transformed into certitude.

The first believers in a new Revelation – for example Peter, who was the first to recognize Jesus, or Mullá Ḥusayn who recognized the Báb – reached certitude through direct knowledge of the Manifestation for that era. Today, the Manifestation Himself being absent, we rely on His Word, the 'Word of God' whose power is just as great:

The Word of God is the master key for the whole world, inasmuch as through its potency the doors of the hearts of men, which in reality are the doors of heaven, are unlocked . . . It is an ocean inexhaustible in riches, comprehending all things. Every thing which can be perceived is but an emanation therefrom. High, immeasurably high is this sublime station, in whose shadow moveth the essence of loftiness and splendour, wrapt in praise and adoration.[6]

In writing this little book I can make no claim to originality – which according to Einstein is in any case no more than knowing how to hide one's sources. Many sources have been cited here. Nevertheless, as Pascal writes in his *Pensées*: 'Let no one say that I have said nothing new: the arrangement of the material is new.'[7] And this ripple of things said and re-said brings originality to the life of the spirit.

It is my hope that what has been proposed here in all humility may be of help in allowing us to see the difficulties of our lives in perspective, and even more important, that it may encourage us to open a window in our hearts through which the Word of God may enter to fill them with love.

> The candle of thine heart is lighted by the hand of My power, quench it not with the contrary winds of self and passion. The healer of all thine ills is remembrance of Me, forget it not. Make My love thy treasure and cherish it even as thy very sight and life.[8]

He who loves the Messengers of God with all his heart and strength holds the keys to the whole world, and above all, to his own heart. This is both the starting point and the point of arrival; everything else follows from this.

> The essence of wealth is love for Me; whoso loveth Me is the possessor of all things, and he that loveth Me not is indeed of the poor and needy. This is that which the Finger of Glory and Splendour hath revealed.[9]

17

. . . AND A CONCLUSION

In taking as a guideline the Báb's prayer 'Is there any Remover of Difficulties save God . . .', this little book has attempted to provide a few reflections on the trials and tribulations we all face, without diminishing their importance or the serious effects they can have on our lives.

Although no one can call into question the gravity of the tests to which we may be subjected, we all know how the lack of a healthy sense of humour can succeed in making such tests even worse. People who are devoid of humour often bring problems on themselves, and also on others, in their lack of understanding for those who are able smile in the face of disaster. This final chapter therefore brings together some considerations on humour.

In the 'Intermezzo' we briefly acknowledged the role that wit, irony and humour can play when life becomes difficult and puts us to the test. Here, we take the opportunity to take up the subject again, without fear of being accused of superficiality. We will share stories drawn from various spiritual traditions which, by integrating humour into their teachings, suggest appropriate responses to tests and difficulties.

Humour forms bonds between human beings; it can de-dramatize a situation by creating detachment from it, which is always a good thing. It's a special kind of human intelligence, essential for the overall balance of an individual in relationship both to himself and to others. It is a gift possessed by those who are pure in heart, who are able to convey profound truths in a light-hearted way, gladdening the heart rather than oppressing it.

'Abdu'l-Bahá always welcomed everyone with a beaming smile, asking them: 'Are you happy?'. 'Be happy! Be happy!' – in recalling these often-repeated words of 'Abdu'l-Bahá, we cannot but experience a profound desire to bring a touch of serenity to the heart of every suffering soul, a radiant smile to every face. How can a face *not* be beautiful when it mirrors the soul – that gem of inestimable value in every one of us, that essence, that particle of God made in His image? A smile is none other than the frame – a refined setting for this precious gem, and can only make it even more beautiful.

In Esslemont's *Bahá'u'lláh and the New Era* we read:

Both at lunch and supper He ['Abdu'l-Bahá] used to entertain a number of pilgrims and friends, and charm His guest with happy and humorous stories as well as precious talks on a great variety of subjects. 'My home is the home of laughter and mirth', He declared, and indeed it was so.[1]

'Abdu'l-Bahá loved laughter and His laughter was often a source of solace. He was blessed with a delightful sense of humour. He found fun in situations and stories. He cited, for example, an anecdote to stress how important proper communication between people is:

I recall an incident which occurred in Baghdad. There were two friends who knew not each other's language. One fell ill, the other visited him, but not being able to express his sympathy in words, resorted to gesture, as if to say, 'How do you feel?'.

With another sign the sick [one] replied, 'I shall soon be dead'; and his visitor, believing the gesture to indicate that he was getting better, said, 'God be praised!'[2]

The Muslim world, and particularly the Sufi tradition, has thousands of humorous stories concerning Mulla Nasrudin, or Nasreddin Hodja (also known as Giufa) that are used to teach spiritual truths. Here is one:

> The Caliph had died and his throne was empty. Giufa went and sat on it. The Grand Vizier ordered the guards to arrest the dervish who had committed such a crime. But Giufa replied: ' I am higher than the Caliph!'
> 'How dare you say such a thing!' exclaimed the amazed Vizier. 'Only the Prophet is higher than the Caliph.'
> 'Well, I'm higher than the Prophet,' continued Giufa, unperturbed.
> 'What? How dare you, miserable sinner! Only God is higher than the Prophet!'
> 'I am even higher than God.'
> 'Infidel!' shouted the Grand Vizier, on the verge of a nervous breakdown. 'Guards! Disembowel that scoundrel immediately! Nothing is higher than God!'
> 'Now you've got it,' said Giufa. 'In fact, I am nothing.'

In the Asian traditions, the parables known as Koan in Zen Buddhism are often used to convey profound truths that lie behind the paradoxical and often ironical character of short jokes or questions shared by the teacher with his students, such as: 'When there's nothing left to do, what do you do?'

In addition, there are also funny stories told by the Tibetan monks, such as the following:

Two monks, one young and one old, are walking together in silence. When they come to the banks of a river they meet a beautiful young girl who asks their help to cross the ford.

To the great astonishment of the younger monk, the older one lifts the woman onto his shoulders and crosses the river. Then the two monks take to the road again in silence.

At the end of the day, the young man asks the elder: 'How could you take that woman on your shoulders when you have made a vow of chastity?' To which the old man replies: 'I carried that woman on my shoulders for a few minutes and then forgot her. But you, after walking all day, are still carrying her in your head!'

Christian theological tradition, so focused on sin and little inclined to humour, is more than compensated in popular Christian wisdom:

Walking in the savannah, a missionary suddenly finds himself facing a roaring lion ready to pounce on him and tear him to pieces. Begging God's help, he prays: 'O Lord, inspire this beast with Christian feelings!'

And a miracle takes place. The lion stops in mid-leap, kneels down, and prays: 'O God! Bless the meal I am about to consume. Amen.'

But the unsurpassed masters of the finest humour are found in the Jewish tradition. Thanks to their keen sense of irony in poking fun at themselves, their own lives and even God, the 'chosen people' have been able to endure centuries of the heavy persecutions that have been heaped upon them due to the divine mission with which they rightly or wrongly consider themselves to be invested. Here is one such story:

Coming out of the synagogue, the rabbi gives thanks to God. He thanks Him for allowing him to have been born one of the chosen people; for choosing him to perform the rites and ceremonies; for giving him faith. He reaffirms that all his adoration and his faith is in Him and Him alone . . . And then, absorbed in this thoughts, he falls into a ravine.

In his fall he manages to grasp a small twig, not a strong branch. Terrified, he shouts: 'Is anyone up there?'

At last a deep voice replies from above: 'My son! I have heard your prayer. Have no fear, let go of the branch. My angels will catch you and gently put you down at the bottom of the cliff.'

Looking at the void beneath his feet, the rabbi asks: 'Is there anyone else up there?'

Throughout history, trials and tribulations have been the daily bread of all the peoples of the world. Earthquakes, tsunamis, floods, famines and epidemics are just some examples of the catastrophic natural events with which man has always lived and that have often disrupted his life but which, thanks to science, he is now learning to dominate. Unfortunately, that same science has also served to produce increasingly sophisticated weapons through which man has brought all kinds of unimaginable suffering to his fellow human beings. According to school curricula it would seem that human history is the story of war, with all that implies: loss of freedom, genocide, persecution, deportation, slavery, and so on and so forth. Entire populations have been oppressed, if not annihilated. Only those who have maintained their identity and cohesion thanks to their fundamental spiritual values (of which the first is faith), have succeeded not only in surviving, but in becoming stronger, even in arousing religious feeling in their oppressors. This has been due to their feelings of love, tolerance and compassion, certainly not to fanaticism; to their sense of wonder at the beauty of works of art and architecture; to being inspired by music and poetry and moved by song; to the thrill of the dance . . . and last but not least, to eliciting joy and harmony thanks to a subtle irony tempered by a keen sense of humour.

Thus concludes our research, although it is by no means exhausted here. Life is a perennial school in which each of us is personally committed through our own experiences, joys and sorrows. We cannot delegate others to live it for us.

But we are not alone! There is a Friend Who watches over us, Who loves us more than we can possibly love each other; Who knows what is good for us and will take our hand if we allow him to. This is the Friend addressed in one of the most beautiful prayers attributed to 'Abdu'l-Bahá: 'O God! Thou art more friend to me than I am to myself.'[3]

As in all true friendship, this too – indeed especially this – requires a counterpart, a commitment on our part. First of all, we need to open our heart to the Friend, or otherwise, as Bahá'u'lláh warns us in the Hidden Words: 'If thou lovest Me not, My love can in no wise reach thee.'[4] Even the most sincere and disinterested Friend must respect our wishes. And so we need to express our deep feelings in compliance with the covenant of friendship: 'I dedicate myself to Thee . . .' because 'Thou art my Guide and my Refuge,' and so, in complete trust, 'I lay all my affairs in Thy hand.'[5]

This is an act of love and courage requiring strength and purity of intent that our Friend will be willing to support us when we turn to Him: 'O God! Refresh and gladden my spirit. Purify my heart. Illumine my powers.'[6]

We may then ask ourselves how we can possibly be overcome by adversity, when:

Whatever hath befallen you, hath been for the sake of God. This is the truth, and in this there is no doubt. You should, therefore, leave all your affairs in His Hands, place your trust in him, and rely upon Him. He will assuredly not forsake you. In this, likewise, there is no doubt. No father will surrender his sons to devouring beasts; no shepherd will leave his flock to ravening wolves. He will most certainly do his utmost to protect his own.[7]

And so, if I have faith in the love of the Friend: 'I will not dwell on the unpleasant things of life . . . I will no longer be full of anxiety, nor will I let trouble harass me,' so that 'I will no longer be sorrowful and grieved,' but '**I will be a happy and joyful being.**'[8]

BIBLIOGRAPHY

'Abdu'l-Bahá. *Paris Talks: Addresses given by 'Abdu'l-Bahá in 1911* (1912). London: Bahá'í Publishing Trust, 12th ed. 1995.

— *The Promulgation of Universal Peace: Talks Delivered by 'Abdu'l-Bahá During His Visit to the United States and Canada in 1912* (1922, 1925). Comp. H. MacNutt. Wilmette, IL: Bahá'í Publishing Trust, 2nd ed. 1982.

— *Selections from the Writings of 'Abdu'l-Bahá*. Comp. Research Department of the Universal House of Justice. Haifa: Bahá'í World Centre, 1978.

— *Some Answered Questions* (1908). Comp. and trans. Laura Clifford Barney. Haifa: Bahá'í World Centre, rev. ed. 2014.

— *Tablets of 'Abdu'l-Bahá* (etext in the Ocean search engine; originally published as *Tablets of Abdul-Baha Abbas*. 3 vols. Chicago: Bahá'í Publishing Society, 1909–1916). Wilmette, IL: National Spiritual Assembly of the Bahá'ís of the United States, 1980.

— *Will and Testament of 'Abdu'l-Bahá*. Wilmette, IL: National Spiritual Assembly of the Bahá'ís of the United States, 1944.

Almaas, H. A. *Diamond Heart: Elements of the Real in Man*. Book 1. Boulder, Colorado: Shambhala, 2000.

The Báb. *Selections from the Writings of the Báb*. Comp. Research Department of the Universal House of Justice. Haifa: Bahá'í World Centre, 1976.

Bahá'í International Community, Office of Public Information. *Who is Writing the Future? Reflections on the Twentieth Century* (1999). Wilmette, IL: Bahá'í Publishing Trust, 2000.

Bahá'í Prayers: A Selection of Prayers Revealed by Bahá'u'lláh, The Báb, and 'Abdu'l-Bahá. Wilmette, IL: Bahá'í Publishing Trust, rev. ed. 1991.

The Bahá'í World. Vol. 1 (*Bahá'í Year Book*, 1925–1926). New York: Bahá'í

Publishing Committee, 1926; vol. XVI ((1973–1976), Haifa: Bahá'í World Centre, 1978).

Bahá'u'lláh. *Epistle to the Son of the Wolf.* Trans. Shoghi Effendi. Wilmette, IL: Bahá'í Publishing Trust, rev. ed. 1976.

— *Gleanings from the Writings of Bahá'u'lláh.* Trans. Shoghi Effendi. Wilmette, IL: Bahá'í Publishing Trust, 2nd ed. 1976.

— *The Hidden Words of Bahá'u'lláh.* Trans. Shoghi Effendi. Wilmette, IL: Bahá'í Publishing Trust, 1970; New Delhi: Bahá'í Publishing Trust, 1987.

— *The Kitáb-i-Aqdas: The Most Holy Book.* Haifa: Bahá'í World Centre, 1992.

— *Kitáb-i-Íqán: The Book of Certitude.* Trans. Shoghi Effendi. Wilmette, IL: Bahá'í Publishing Trust, 2nd ed. 1950, 1981.

— *Prayers and Meditations by Bahá'u'lláh.* Trans. Shoghi Effendi. Wilmette, IL: Bahá'í Publishing Trust, 1938, 1987.

— *The Seven Valleys and the Four Valleys.* Trans. M. Gail with A-K.Khan. Wilmette, IL: Bahá'í Publishing Trust, rev. ed. 1975.

— *The Summons of the Lord of Hosts: Tablets of Bahá'u'lláh.* Haifa: Bahá'í World Centre, 2002.

— *Tablets of Bahá'u'lláh Revealed after the Kitáb-i-Aqdas.* Comp. Research Department of the Universal House of Justice. Haifa: Bahá'í World Centre, 1978.

Bausani, Alessandro. *Saggi sulla Fede Baha'i.* Rome: Casa Editrice Bahá'í, 1991.

Boni, Cesare. *Dove Va l'Anima dopo la Morte* [Where the soul goes after death]. Turin: Amrita, 2011.

Buber, Martin. *Tales of the Hasidim.* Trans. Olga Marx. New York: Schocken Books, 1947, 1991.

The Compilation of Compilations. Prepared by the Universal House of Justice 1963–1990. 2 vols. Sydney: Bahá'í Publications Australia, 1991.

Dacquino, Giacomo. *Dove Incontri l'Anima: Pscicologia, Spiritualitá e Vita Quotidiana* [Where You Meet the Soul: Psychology, Spirituality and Daily Life]. Milan: Mondadori 2011

The Divine Art of Living: Selections from the Bahá'í Writings. Comp. Mabel Hyde Paine. Wilmette, IL: Bahá'í Publishing Trust, 4th rev. ed. 1979.

Einstein, Albert. *The World As I See It* (1949). Seattle: Citadel, 2006.

Esslemont, J. E. *Bahá'u'lláh and the New Era*. Wilmette IL: Bahá'í Publishing Trust, 1980.

Gibran, Khalil. *The Prophet*. London: Heinemann, 1964.

Heschel, Abraham J. *The Prophets*. New York: Harper, 1969.

Hillman, James. *The Dream and the Underworld*. New York: HarperCollins, 1979.

Laszlo, Ervin. *You Can Change the World: The Global Citizen's Handbook for Living on Planet Earth*. A Report of the Club of Budapest. Select Books, 2003.

Lights of Guidance: A Bahá'í Reference File. Comp. H. Hornby. New Delhi: Bahá'í Publishing Trust, 5th ed. 1997.

Littleword, Stephen. *Piccole Cose*. Rimini: Il Giardino dei Libri, 2013.

Manzoni, Alessandro. *I Promessi Sposi* [The Betrothed]. Ed. Charles W. Eliot, in The Harvard Classics, vol. 21. New York: P. F. Collier, 1909. Online version.

Nabíl-i-A'zam (Muḥammad-i-Zarandí). *The Dawn-Breakers: Nabíl's Narrative of the Early Days of the Bahá'í Revelation*. Trans. Shoghi Effendi. Wilmette, IL: Bahá'í Publishing Trust, 1932.

Nietzsche, Friedrich. *The Gay Science*. Ed. Bernard Williams. Cambridge Texts in the History of Philosophy. Cambridge: Cambridge University Press, 2001.

Pascal, Blaise. *Pensées*. London: Penguin Classics, 1995. Also available online at e.g. www.gutenberg.org.

Principles of Bahá'í Administration: A Compilation. London: Bahá'í Publishing Trust, 1950.

Proust, Marcel. *In Search of Lost Time*. Trans. Lydia Davis et al. London: Allen Lane, 2002.

Rabbani, Rúḥíyyih. *Prescription for Living*. Oxford: George Ronald, 2nd rev. ed. 1978.

Savi, Julio. *The Eternal Quest for God: An Introduction to the Divine Philosophy of 'Abdu'l-Bahá*. Oxford: George Ronald, 1989. Translated from *Nell'Universo sulle Tracce di Dio*. Rome: Editrice Nur, 1988.

Scarcia Amoretti, Biancamaria (ed.). *Il Corano: Una Lettura*. Rome: Carocci, 2009.

Shoghi Effendi. *The Advent of Divine Justice* (1939). Wilmette, IL: Bahá'í Publishing Trust, 1984.

— *Directives from the Guardian*. Comp. Gertrude Garrida. New Delhi: Bahá'í Publishing Trust, 1973.

— *God Passes By* (1944). Wilmette, IL: Bahá'í Publishing Trust, rev. ed. 1974.

Star of the West: The Bahai Magazine. Periodical, 25 vols. 1910–1935. Vols. 1–14 RP Oxford: George Ronald, 1978. Complete CD-ROM version: Talisman Educational Software/Special Ideas, 2001.

Taherzadeh, Adib. *The Revelation of Bahá'u'lláh*. 4 vols. Oxford: George Ronald, 1974–1987.

Thoreau, Henry David. *Walden, or, Life in the Woods*. Boston: Ticknor and Fields, 1854. Many editions online.

Tod, Ginny. *Overcoming Difficulties*. Oxford: George Ronald, 2003.

The Universal House of Justice. Message to the Bahá'ís of the World, Riḍván 150 (1993). Available online.

Weil, Henry. *Closer than your Life Vein*. Anchorage: National Spiritual Assembly of the Baha'is of Alaska, 1978.

Zuffada, Luigi. *L'Antico dei Giorni* [The Ancient of Days]. Vol. I. Rome: Casa Editrice Bahá'í, 1989.

— *Il Maestro* [The Master]. Rome: Casa Editrice Bahá'í, 1982.

NOTES AND REFERENCES

Page xi

1 Bahá'u'lláh, *Gleanings from the Writings of Bahá'u'lláh*, LXVI, p. 129.
2 Bahá'u'lláh, Súriy-i-Muluk (Tablet to the Kings), in Bahá'u'lláh, *The Summons of the Lord of Hosts*, p. 195.

Prologue: A Brief History

1 Excerpts from Luigi Zuffada, *L'Antico dei Giorni* and *Il Maestro*.
2 Bahá'u'lláh, *Gleanings from the Writings of Bahá'u'lláh*, CLI, pp. 319–20.
3 ibid. XXVI, p. 62.
4 ibid. VII, pp. 10–11.

Introduction

1 Nabíl, *The Dawn-Breakers*, pp. 191–2.

1. Some Initial Considerations

1 Bahá'u'lláh, *Gleanings from the Writings of Bahá'u'lláh*, LXXI, p. 138.
2 Bahá'u'lláh, *The Kitáb-i-Aqdas*, para. 43, p. 35.
3 From a letter written on behalf of Shoghi Effendi, in *Directives from the Guardian*, no. 160, p. 60; also in most Bahá'í prayer books as an introduction to the Tablet of Ahmad.
4 Nabíl, *The Dawn-Breakers*, p. 192.
5 Bahá'u'lláh, Tablet of Ahmad, in most Bahá'í prayer books.
6 Letter written on behalf of Shoghi Effendi, 6 March 1937, in *Lights of Guidance*, no. 1517.
7 Letter written on behalf of the Universal House of Justice to a National Spiritual Assembly, 24 November 1971, in *Lights of Guidance*, no. 1528.
8 Bahá'u'lláh, quoted in Shoghi Effendi, *God Passes By*, p. 119.

9   Letter written on behalf of the Universal House of Justice to the National Spiritual Assembly of Bolivia, 16 October 1979, in *Lights of Guidance*, no. 1573.

10   Letter written on behalf of Shoghi Effendi to an individual believer, 26 November 1939, in *Lights of Guidance*, no. 1511.

2. The Creative Power of the Word of God

1   Taherzadeh, *The Revelation of Bahá'u'lláh*, vol. 1, p. 30.
2   Bahá'u'lláh, *Gleanings from the Writings of Bahá'u'lláh*, LXXII, pp. 141–2.
3   Taherzadeh, *The Revelation of Bahá'u'lláh*, vol. 1, pp. 31–2.
4   'Abdu'l-Bahá, *Tablets*, vol. 3, p. 683.

3. The Power and Purpose of Prayer

1   Quoted by Bahá'u'lláh, *The Seven Valleys*, p. 22.
2   Taherzadeh, *The Revelation of Bahá'u'lláh*, vol. 2, p. 232.
3   Bahá'u'lláh, *Prayers and Meditations*, XXXVIII, p. 54.
4   Taherzadeh, *The Revelation of Bahá'u'lláh*, vol. 2, p. 232.
5   Bahá'u'lláh, quoted in *The Bahá'í World*, vol. 1, p. 42; Also in *The Divine Art of Living*, p. 71.
6   Bahá'u'lláh, *Gleanings from the Writings of Bahá'u'lláh*, CLII, pp. 322–3.
7   Savi, *The Eternal Quest for God*, p. 121.
8   Bahá'u'lláh, *Gleanings from the Writings of Bahá'u'lláh*, I, pp. 4–5.
9   Bahá'u'lláh, *Kitáb-i-Íqán*, pp. 194–5.
10   Taherzadeh, *The Revelation of Bahá'u'lláh*, vol. II, pp. 232–3.
11   Bahá'u'lláh, *Prayers and Meditations*, LVI, pp. 82–3.
12   Taherzadeh, *The Revelation of Bahá'u'lláh*, vol. 2, p. 233.
13   Bahá'u'lláh, quoted in *The Bahá'í World*, vol. 1, p. 42; Also in *The Divine Art of Living*, p. 71.
14   Bahá'u'lláh, *Prayers and Meditations*, LVI, p. 83.

4. More on Prayer

1   Bahá'u'lláh, *Gleanings from the Writings of Bahá'u'lláh*, CXXXVI, p. 295.
2   ibid.
3   Bahá'u'lláh, *Kitáb-i-Aqdas*, para. 182, p. 85.
4   Matt. 6: 5–6.
5   'Abdu'l-Bahá, quoted in Esslemont, *Bahá'u'lláh and the New Era*, p. 89.
6   See *Principles of Bahá'í Administration*, pp. 90–91.
7   Bahá'u'lláh, *Gleanings from the Writings of Bahá'u'lláh*, CXXXIV, p. 290.

8   Bahá'u'lláh, *Hidden Words*, Arabic no. 18.
9   Bahá'u'lláh, quoted in Shoghi Effendi, *The Advent of Divine Justice*, p. 65.
10   The Báb, Persian Bayán VII:19, in *Selections from the Writings of the Báb*, p. 78.
11   Bahá'u'lláh, *Gleanings from the Writings of Bahá'u'lláh*, CXXV, p. 265.
12   ibid. CXXXVI, p. 295.
13   'Abdu'l-Bahá, *Paris Talks*, no. 6, para. 12, p. 20
14   'Abdu'l-Bahá, *Selections from the Writings of 'Abdu'l-Bahá*, no. 150, p. 178.
15   Boni, *Dove Va l'Anima dopo la Morte*, p. 93.
16   'Abdu'l-Bahá, *Selections from the Writings of 'Abdu'l-Bahá*, no. 22, p. 51.
17   Bahá'u'lláh, Lawḥ-i-Aqdas, in *Tablets of Bahá'u'lláh Revealed after the Kitáb-i-Aqdas*, p. 16.
18   Bahá'u'lláh, in *Bahá'í Prayers*, no. 33, p. 40.
19   The Báb, in *Bahá'í Prayers*, no. 2, p. 7.
20   ibid. no. 3, p. 7.
21   The Báb, excerpt from the Dalá'il-i-Sab'ih, in *Selections from the Writings of the Báb*, p. 123.

5. The Purpose of Difficulties and of Overcoming Them

1   The first two pages of this chapter draw on Ginny Tod's Foreword to her book *Overcoming Difficulties*.
2   Bahá'u'lláh, *Epistle to the Son of the Wolf*, p. 17.
3   Bahá'u'lláh, *Hidden Words*, Arabic no. 51.
4   Abridged from Tod, *Overcoming Difficulties*, pp. vii–viii.
5   Bahá'u'lláh, *Gleanings from the Writings of Bahá'u'lláh*, LXXVII, p. 149.
6   ibid. XXVII, pp. 65–6.
7   Tod, *Overcoming Difficulties*, p. viii.
8   Bahá'u'lláh, quoted in Shoghi Effendi, *The Advent of Divine Justice*, p. 69.
9   Manzoni, *The Betrothed*, Ch. 8, para. 84.
10   Yehudah Zevi of Stretyn, 'Bitter, Not Bad', in Buber, *Tales of the Hasidim*.
11   Bahá'u'lláh, *Kitáb-i-Aqdas*, paras. 40, 43, pp. 34–5.
12   'Abdu'l-Bahá, *Tablets*, vol. 1, pp. 12–13.
13   Bahá'u'lláh, *Gleanings from the Writings of Bahá'u'lláh*, V, pp. 7–8.
14   'Abdu'l-Bahá, *Selections from the Writings of 'Abdu'l-Bahá*, no. 197, p. 239.
15   Bahá'u'lláh, *Gleanings from the Writings of Bahá'u'lláh*, CIX, p. 215.
16   ibid. CXXVIII, p. 276.

17 Bahá'u'lláh, *Seven Valleys*, p. 35.
18 Bahá'u'lláh, *Gleanings from the Writings of Bahá'u'lláh*, CLIII, pp. 328–9.
19 'Abdu'l-Bahá, *Selections from the Writings of 'Abdu'l-Bahá*, no. 1, p. 3.
20 Bahá'u'lláh, Kalimát-i-Firdawsíyyih, in *Tablets of Bahá'u'lláh Revealed after the Kitáb-i-Aqdas*, p. 57.
21 'Abdu'l-Bahá, *Paris Talks*, no. 14, p. 43.
22 'Abdu'l-Bahá, in *Star of the West*, vol. VIII, no. 19 (2 March 1918), p. 240.
23 'Abdu'l-Bahá, *Paris Talks*, no. 57, p. 191.
24 Bahá'u'lláh, *Kitáb-i-Íqán*, para. 8, p. 8.
25 'Abdu'l-Bahá, *Paris Talks*, no. 57, p. 191.
26 Bahá'u'lláh, *Gleanings from the Writings of Bahá'u'lláh*, LII, pp. 106–7.

6. Types of Affliction

1 Rabbani, *Prescription for Living*, pp. 129–31.
2 Dacquino, *Dove Incontri l'Anima*, p. 169.
3 ibid. p. 142.
4 Matt. 26:39.
5 Buber, *Tales of the Hasidim*, pp. 410–11.
6 Bahá'u'lláh, *Hidden Words*, Arabic no. 51.
7 Bahá'u'lláh, *Gleanings from the Writings of Bahá'u'lláh*, LII, p. 106.
8 Bahá'u'lláh, Lawḥ-i-Ḥikmat, in *Tablets of Bahá'u'lláh Revealed after the Kitáb-i-Aqdas*, p. 138.
9 The authorship of this story is disputed, attributed to various different people. The version quoted here is that attributed to Mary Stevenson, available on www. footprints-inthe-sand.com.
10 Nabíl, *The Dawn-Breakers*, pp. 92–3.
11 'Abdu'l-Bahá, *The Promulgation of Universal Peace*, p. 328.
12 Savi, *The Eternal Quest for God*, pp. 229–30.
13 Keats, 'Ode on a Grecian Urn'.
14 'Abdu'l-Bahá, *Tablets*, vol. II, p. 460.
15 Quoted in Paolo Coelho, 'The Tale of the Ancient Alchemists', Postcript in Laszlo, *You Can Change the World*.

7. The Mystery of Sacrifice

1 'Abdu'l-Bahá, *The Promulgation of Universal Peace*, pp. 449–52.
2 ibid.

God Loves Laughter

1 Anonymous, sometimes ascribed to Jiddu Krishnamurti.
2 Bahá'u'lláh, Ṭarázát, in *Tablets of Bahá'u'lláh Revealed after the Kitáb-i-Aqdas*, p. 35.
3 Bahá'u'lláh, *Gleanings*, CXXXIV, p. 289.

4   Attributed to 'Abdu'l-Bahá.
5   Victor Hugo 'A Villequier': 'Peut-être faites-vous des choses incon-
    nues/Où la douleur de l'homme entre comme élément./Peut-être
    est-il utile à vos desseins sans nombre . . .' ; referred to in Bausani,
    Saggi sulla Fede Bahá'í, p. 41.
6   Bahá'u'lláh, *Gleanings*, LXVI, pp. 128–9.
7   The title of a book by Hand of the Cause William Sears.
8   As explained by Claudio Magris in an article in *Corriere della Sera*, 24
    November 2005.
9   See for example Einstein, *The World As I See It*.
10 Gen. 31:24–31.
11 Bausani, *Saggi sulla Fede Bahá'í*, pp. 42, 43, 208.
12 See Hillman, *The Dream and the Underworld*.
13 Joyce, *Ulysses*, Chapter 3.
14 Buber, *Tales of the Hasidim*.
15 Heschel, *The Prophets*.
16 Bahá'u'lláh, *Hidden Words*, Arabic no. 5.
17 Bahá'u'lláh, short Obligatory Prayer.
18 Thoreau, Conclusion to *Walden*.
19 'Abdu'l-Bahá, *Selections from the Writings of 'Abdu'l-Bahá*, no. 17, p.
    35.
20 Bahá'u'lláh, in *The Compilation of Compilations*, vol. II, no. 2050, p.
    337.
21 Letter on behalf of Shoghi Effendi to the National Spiritual Assembly
    of the Bahá'ís of the United States, 21 September 1957, in *Lights of
    Guidance*, no. 454.
22 Letter from Shoghi Effendi to the Spiritual Assembly of Tehran, 30
    October 1924, ibid. no. 457.
23 Nietzsche, *The Gay Science*, Book 3, no. 173, p. 136.

8. To Praise God

1   Bahá'u'lláh, *Prayers and Meditations*, CLXXVI, p. 272.
2   ibid. LXXXVIII, p. 149.
3   ibid. CXIV, pp. 194–5.
4   Bahá'u'lláh, *Tablets of Bahá'u'lláh Revealed after the Kitáb-i-Aqdas*, pp.
    262–3.

9. Overcoming Difficulties

1   Stephen Littleword, *Piccole Cose*.
2   Bahá'u'lláh, *Hidden Words*, Arabic no. 18.
3   Bahá'u'lláh, *Prayers and Meditations*, CX, p. 186.
4   Bahá'u'lláh, *The Seven Valleys*, p. 22.
5   ibid.

6   ibid. p. 9.
7   ibid. p. 58 (from *The Four Valleys*).
8   Bahá'u'lláh, *Gleanings from the Writings of Bahá'u'lláh*, LXXI, p. 138.
9   Bahá'u'lláh, *The Kitáb-i-Aqdas*, para. 43, p. 35.
10 Bahá'u'lláh, *Gleanings from the Writings of Bahá'u'lláh*, LXXXVIII, p. 175.
11 Bahá'u'lláh, *Epistle to the Son of the Wolf*, p. 134.
12 Bahú'lláh, *Prayers and Meditations*, LXVI, p. 108.
13 Bahá'u'lláh, *Gleanings from the Writings of Bahá'u'lláh*, CXIV, p. 239.
14 ibid. LXVI, p. 129.
15 ibid. CXXXIV, p. 290.
16 The Báb, quoted in Nabíl, *The Dawn-Breakers*, p. 94.

10. The Value of Struggle

1   'Abdu'l-Bahá, *Some Answered Questions*, no. 3, paras. 1 and 9, pp. 8, 10.
2   Bahá'u'lláh, *The Seven Valleys*, p. 40.
3   See Almaas : *Diamond Heart : Elements of the Real in Man*.
4   Qur'án 49: 15 (Rodwell translation).
5   See Scarcia Amoretti, *Il Corano: Una Lettura*, pp. 169–70.
6   Rabbani, *Prescription for Living*, pp. 70–71.
7   ibid.

11. Service

1   See for example Weil, *Closer than your Life Vein*.
2   'Abdu'l-Bahá, quoted in *Star of the West*, XIII, p. 112.
3   Bahá'u'lláh, quoted in Shoghi Effendi, *The Advent of Divine Justice*, p. 70.
4   Bahá'u'lláh, *The Seven Valleys*, p. 22.
5   'Abdu'l-Bahá, *Selections from the Writings of 'Abdu'l-Bahá*, no. 162, p. 192.
6   Savi, *Nell'Universo sulle Tracce di Dio*, p. 287.
7   Bahá'u'lláh, quoted in Shoghi Effendi, *The Advent of Divine Justice*, p. 65.
8   Bahá'u'lláh, *Gleanings from the Writings of Bahá'u'lláh*, CXXVIII, p. 278.
9   Bahá'u'lláh, *The Seven Valleys*, pp. 21–2.
10 Bahá'u'lláh, *Gleanings from the Writings of Bahá'u'lláh*, CXXX, p. 285.
11 Bahá'u'lláh, Lawḥ-i-Ḥikmat, in *Tablets of Bahá'u'lláh Revealed after the Kitáb-i-Aqdas*, p. 138.
12 Bahá'u'lláh, *Gleanings from the Writings of Bahá'u'lláh*, XCVI, p. 196.
13 The Báb's Address to the Letters of the Living, quoted in Nabíl, *The Dawn-Breakers*, p. 92.

14 'Abdu'l-Bahá, *Selections from the Writings of 'Abdu'l-Bahá*, no. 210, pp. 266–7.
15 'Abdu'l-Bahá, *Will and Testament*, para. 53.
16 Bahá'u'lláh, *Gleanings from the Writings of Bahá'u'lláh*, CLVIII, p. 335.
17 ibid. CXLIV, p. 314.
18 Bahá'u'lláh, *Tablets of Bahá'u'lláh Revealed after the Kitáb-i-Aqdas*, p. 242.
19 Bahá'u'lláh, *Gleanings from the Writings of Bahá'u'lláh*, CXXIX, p. 280.
20 Bahá'u'lláh, *Tablets of Bahá'u'lláh Revealed after the Kitáb-i-Aqdas*, p. 256.

12. Obedience and Submission

1 'Abdu'l-Bahá, in 'Life in the Most Great Prison', in *Star of the West*, vol. 8, no. 13 (4 Nov.1917), p. 172.
2 Bahá'u'lláh, *Gleanings from the Writings of Bahá'u'lláh*, CLIII, p. 329.
3 Paraphrased from Proust, *In Search of Lost Time*, vol. 5, ch. 2, 'The Prisoner'.
4 The Universal House of Justice, Message to the Bahá'ís of the World, Riḍván 150 (1993), para. 8.
5 Bahá'u'lláh, *Gleanings from the Writings of Bahá'u'lláh*, CXXV, p. 268.
6 Bahá'u'lláh, *Hidden Words*, Persian no. 19.

13. Joy and Pain

1 Bahá'u'lláh, *Gleanings from the Writings of Bahá'u'lláh*, LXXXII, p. 160.
2 For further information see Bahá'u'lláh, *Gleanings from the Writings of Bahá'u'lláh;* 'Abdu'l-Bahá, *Some Answered Questions,* and other Bahá'í texts.
3 'Abdu'l-Bahá, *Paris Talks*, no. 6, para. 7, p. 19.
4 Bahá'u'lláh, *Gleanings from the Writings of Bahá'u'lláh*, XI, p. 15.
5 Bahá'u'lláh, *The Seven Valleys*, p. 29.
6 'Abdu'l-Bahá, *Paris Talks*, no. 35, para. 1, p. 110.
7 Gibran, *The Prophet*, pp. 36–7.
8 'Abdu'l-Bahá, *Paris Talks*, no. 35, para. 2, p. 110.
9 Letter on behalf of Shoghi Effendi to an individual, 15 October 1952, in *Lights of Guidance*, no. 381.
10 'Abdu'l-Bahá, quoted in *The Bahá'í World*, vol. XVI, p. 40.

14. The Path that Leads to Happiness

1 Bahá'í International Community, *Who is Writing the Future?*, section IV. It may be useful here to recall: 'Self has really two meanings: one is self, the identity of the individual created by God. This is the self mentioned in such passages as 'he hath known God who hath known

himself etc.'. The other self is the ego, the dark, animalistic heritage each one of us has, the lower nature that can develop into a monster of selfishness, brutality, lust and so on' (Letter on behalf of Shoghi Effendi to an individual, 10 December 1947, in *Lights of Guidance*, no. 386).

2   Bahá'u'lláh, *Gleanings from the Writings of Bahá'u'lláh*, XCVI, p. 196.
3   'Abdu'l-Bahá, *Tablets*, vol. 2, pp. 459–60.
4   Rabbani, *Prescription for Living*, p. 62.
5   Bahá'u'lláh, *Hidden Words*, Arabic no. 1.
6   'Abdu'l-Bahá, *Selections from the Writings of 'Abdu'l-Bahá*, no. 1, p. 3.
7   ibid. pp. 244–5.
8   Rabbani, *Prescription for Living*, p. 63.
9   Bahá'u'lláh, Lawḥ-i-Dunyá, in *Tablets of Bahá'u'lláh Revealed after the Kitáb-i-Aqdas*, p. 88.
10 Rabbani, *Prescription for Living*, p. 67.
11 ibid. p. 71.
12 Bahá'u'lláh, quoted in *The Compilation of Compilations*, vol. 1, no. 1020, p. 460.
13 Rabbani, *Prescription for Living*, p. 72.
14 'Abdu'l-Bahá, *Paris Talks*, no. 23, p. 68.
15 Bahá'u'lláh, *Gleanings from the Writings of Bahá'u'lláh*, CXXXIII, p. 289.
16 'Abdu'l-Bahá, *Tablets*, vol. 1, p. 61.
17 Bahá'u'lláh, *Gleanings from the Writings of Bahá'u'lláh*, CXVII, p. 250.
18 'Abdu'l-Bahá, *Paris Talks*, no. 55, p. 189.
19 'Abdu'l-Bahá, *The Promulgation of Universal Peace*, p. 453.

15. Is There Room for Doubt?

1   See Dacquino, *Dove Incontri l'Anima*, pp. 166, 187–91. Giacomo Dacquino is a psychiatrist well known as the author of numerous books and a speaker at national and international conferences. He teaches at the University of Torino.
2   Bahá'u'lláh, *Gleanings from the Writings of Bahá'u'lláh*, CLX, p. 338.
3   Bahá'u'lláh, *Hidden Words*, Arabic no. 51.
4   Bahá'u'lláh, *The Seven Valleys*, p. 36.
5   ibid. pp. 8, 11.
6   ibid. p. 40.

16. A Short Summing Up . . .

1   Bahá'u'lláh, *Gleanings from the Writings of Bahá'u'lláh*, CXXX, p. 285.
2   ibid. II, p. 5.
3   ibid. LXXXIX, p. 176.
4   Bahá'u'lláh, *The Seven Valleys*, p. 22.
5   Bahá'u'lláh, *Prayers and Meditations*, LVI, p. 83.

6 Bahá'u'lláh, Lawḥ-i-Maqṣúd, in *Tablets of Bahá'u'lláh Revealed after the Kitáb-i-Aqdas*, p. 173.
7 Pascal, *Pensées*, no. 2.
8 Bahá'u'lláh, *Hidden Words*, Persian no. 32.
9 Bahá'u'lláh, Words of Wisdom, in *Tablets of Bahá'u'lláh Revealed after the Kitáb-i-Aqdas*, p. 156.

17. . . . and a Conclusion

1 Esslemont, *Bahá'u'lláh and the New Era*, p. 77.
2 *Star of the West*, vol. IV, p. 35.
3 Attributed to 'Abdu'l-Bahá. Regarding the authenticity of this prayer, see bahai-library.com/uhj_authenticity_refresh_spirit.
4 Bahá'u'lláh, *Hidden Words*, Arabic no. 5.
5 Attributed to 'Abdu'l-Bahá.
6 ibid.
7 Bahá'u'lláh, quoted in *The Bahá'í World*, vol. XVIII, p. 10.
8 Attributed to 'Abdu'l-Bahá.

ABOUT THE AUTHOR

It all began with a family – a family like so many others, with good principles and the usual shortcomings. Parents and three children. Enrico is the middle child. Born and brought up on African soil, breathing in the warmth of that land and embedded in it.

A biology graduate, he becomes a secondary school teacher. Married, the father of two children.

Introspective, he is able to communicate his innermost feelings and to correlate them with meticulous study and true knowledge.

Adelisa Ballerio

www.ingramcontent.com/pod-product-compliance
Lightning Source LLC
LaVergne TN
LVHW011237080426
835509LV00005B/538